AF696727

Stolen Justice:

One Woman's Struggle over Race-Bias, Corporate Greed, and Legal Malpractice

Stolen Justice:

One Woman's Struggle over Race-Bias, Corporate Greed, and Legal Malpractice

By

Tseghe M. Foote

Stolen Justice
One Woman's Struggle over Race-Bias, Corporate Greed, and Legal Malpractice

© 2000, Tseghe M. Foote, rev. 2008
All rights reserved

A Stolen Justice Publication.

No part of this book may be used or reproduced in any manner whatsoever without written permission except in the case of brief quotations embodied in critical articles and reviews. For information, please contact:

Stolen Justice, L.L.C.
www.stolenjustice.com
info@stolenjustice.com

Managing Editor: Cassy Matthews, Quill Pen Communications
Cover Design: BookMasters, Inc.
Interior Design: BookMasters, Inc.
Cover Photo by: Glenn Covalli

ISBN: 978-0-9701776-0-5

Printed in the United States of America

Table of Contents

This book is dedicated to

The twelve jurors, eleven white and one black, for believing in me and for sending a strong message to corporate America: No matter how large a corporation you are, you are not immune to punishment if you get caught using your power to discriminate

Democracy and the United States justice system—"For the people by the people"

All civil rights lawyers fighting to secure our social justice and civil rights—you are making a difference.

Those whose goodness leads them to do good things—especially Jana Thorpe for doing the right thing.

I want to thank all of you who have supported me through this difficult time.

My family and friends for giving me the strength to see myself through this fight;

to all the media for reporting the events; and

to all the people who have helped me put this book together.

Author's Note

When I had the Africa House, it was my passion and it came from my heart. Now, since I've been forced to close the store, I've found a new passion and love—to work on social change in the areas of civil rights, women's issues, welfare of immigrants, and small business owners.

Our deepest fear is not that we are inadequate.
Our deepest fear is that we are powerful beyond measure.
It is our light, not our darkness, that most frightens us.
We ask ourselves, "Who am I to be
brilliant, gorgeous, talented, fabulous?"
Actually, who are you NOT to be?
You are a child of God.
Your playing small does not serve the world.
There is nothing enlightened about shrinking
so that other people won't feel insecure around you.
We were born to make manifest the glory of God
that is within us. It is not just in some of us.
It is in everyone. And as we let our own light shine
we unconsciously give other people
permission to do the same.
As we are liberated from our own fear,
our presence automatically liberates others.

—Nelson Mandela, Acceptance Speech

Chapter 1

Down for the Count

In the house of the coward there is no weeping.
—Pedi

I was standing in the back room of Africa House. I knew there were customers out front, but I couldn't face them. I had started to cry again and this time it wouldn't stop. It would never stop again. The world around me closed in and a pain ripped through me that threw me to the floor. My breathing became shallow and ragged, narrowing the sobs into a high-pitched scream at the back of my throat. A hand touched me on the shoulder and a voice came from far away.

When I woke up in the hospital, I learned that a customer looking for assistance had found me on the floor of my office and called security. An ambulance was summoned to transport me to the emergency room. I had had an acute anxiety attack brought on by stress. I spent the rest of the day in the ER, as various nurses checked my blood pressure, monitored my heart, and checked my IV. When it appeared that I had stabilized, my doctor came in to talk to me. "Tseghe, this is serious," he said as he perched at the foot of my bed. "Your body is in distress and if you don't take some serious measures, stress is going to kill you."

For over a year and a half I had been at the mercy of a court system that had been stringing me along like a fish with a hook stuck in its mouth. I never knew from one day to the next whether my dreams would be ended and I would lose everything, or if I would emerge victorious from the fight of my life. It had been a ballet in slow motion. A boxing match with jab after jab. Two fighters dancing back and forth, circling each other in the ring, sizing up the competition. Every day since October of 1996, I had been on edge wondering if the next phone call would mean that it had all been for nothing. That my case was being dismissed and they would win. How could someone live like that?

"It's like a drip of water hitting concrete," the doctor said. "Eventually the water will cause a crack in the concrete that will keep getting wider with every drip. You already have a crack and we have to turn off the water."

My friends had drifted away, one by one. It was too hard for anyone to take, to even fathom. The other store owners in the mall had turned away, too. They didn't want to get involved. Making matters worse, the constant media coverage kept interest in the story high, giving customers a reason to ask me about it daily. It was eating me alive.

The next day, I started seeing a psychiatrist for the first time in my life. Before it all started, I had hardly ever even been to a doctor or taken an aspirin. Now I had to take antidepressants to survive. My hair had started to fall out and the complexion I had always been complimented on now had a sallow tinge to it and clung to the hollows under my cheekbones. I had lost weight and never had an appetite any more. All of my size two clothes had started to hang loosely from my diminishing frame. I had always had such a positive outlook on life, but lately I just wanted to die. As much as I wanted to fight, my body couldn't hold it together for me any more. I had to take action to save myself. I still had my dreams, after all. My father's words called out to me, "If you work hard, you will succeed." Yes, Dad, I will.

Chapter 2

Cinderella Story

Not where I was born, but where it goes well with me is my home.

—Kanuri

The region of Tigray is located in the northeasternmost corner of landlocked Ethiopia on the continent of Africa. It slopes off to the Denakil Desert to the east and its belly holds the country's highest peak, Ras Dashen, at 15,158 feet. The land is rugged and fertile, and temperatures hover in the 60s for most of the year. The people are self-sufficient and proud of their culture. It is a country of fighters who have struggled for centuries to maintain their independence and preserve the integrity of the land.

Despite the strife of the Ethiopian people overall, my childhood there was happy. I was the fourth of eight children, three girls and five boys. My mother stayed at home with us and ran the household. She was a strict disciplinarian, and we didn't dare to cross her. We were a team, after all, and we had plenty of love and respect for each other. Family was the most important thing to us and we all were expected to contribute and share in the responsibilities of making our house a home. We were an average family trying to do the best we could under adverse circumstances.

My father built our house before I was born and we loved it. It was a stone structure with six bedrooms and sat not far from town behind a gate. We had a nice yard to play in and could walk to school. We also had the help of two servants who lived with us. One took care of the laundry produced by our large family and the other prepared all of our meals. We had most of the amenities an average American family would have; the main difference was our lack of wealth as a country, which meant dirt roads and a "waste not, want not" mentality.

My father was an architect and contractor whose perfectionism made him a success. He was known to have a building in progress leveled if he saw an imperfection. It was so much more important to him to build something right than to do it quickly. Our culture was very focused on building structures to last because our country didn't have money to waste. My father practiced this philosophy by creating foundations and structures that will live on in Ethiopia for many decades to come.

The buildings my father created were mostly churches and hospitals, and that was a source of pride for us all. According to historical accounts,

Christianity was founded in Ethiopia and has been the foundation of the culture for many centuries. The country as a whole was very focused on maintaining the purity of this religion by keeping outside influences out as much as possible. As a result, we were very devout Christians and the churches my father built were a symbol of faith to us. To this day, he is known throughout the region as the church builder.

This pride of work was a fundamental lesson that was consistently emphasized throughout my childhood. It was a work ethic that affected us all. We saw our father make a name for himself through hard work and skill. "If you work hard, you will be a success in what you do." My father was the living example of that to us.

Along with that success came sharing. My father was heavily involved in helping the poor—the people so many saw on TV during the droughts in Ethiopia. He started organizations to feed, clothe, and even bury them when the time came. He felt that everyone deserved an equal shot and wanted to help out those who hadn't had the advantages we had.

On religious holidays, the poor from our province were invited to our house for celebration. We would set up tents, have music, and give out food to anyone who came. Our house would become filled with activity and excitement before these events. We would all work together to make it a special and festive day. The people who came were always so grateful to us and it left an unforgettable mark on us all. As children, we learned the importance of charity and treating everyone as equals, no matter how diverse our lives may be.

Unlike my mother, who did not have the opportunity to attend school since she was a female, school consumed my life. My mother insisted on us having the same opportunities as the boys and encouraged us to be self-sufficient and educated. The school we all attended served a population of about 25,000. We started school at the age of five or six and quickly got involved in the popular sports of running or gymnastics. In addition to our studies, the boys were always encouraged to learn the trade of their father and the girls were expected to help out at home. That was just the way it was and we didn't question it. In our strict household, dating wasn't encouraged, but we did social things with friends and focused on our schoolwork and chores at home.

We learned the basic economic principle of supply and demand in the ninth grade, and that was about the time that my dream of owning my own business started to form. My father had made a lasting impression already and I wanted to be a success like him.

Another influential piece of my childhood was my constant contact with the Americans who worked in Ethiopia in the Peace Corps. The organization was created in 1961 to promote world peace and friendship. These American volunteers perform social and humanitarian service overseas and were very active in Ethiopia. With education as a primary focus for the organization, many of our teachers were American. I was enamored with them immediately. I found ways to ingratiate myself with them—and teaching them the native tongue of our province was one.

Our entire family was very involved with the Peace Corps workers in the spirit of supporting their cause. My father even rented apartments to many of the volunteers in a building that he owned. This gave me more reason to be near them and observe them. I was fascinated by the fact that they had come to a strange place simply to help. Their hard work was familiar to me and inspired me further. My drive for independence was fueled under the influence of these Americans. I decided then that my dream of owning a business would include moving to America to do it.

The Americans I observed in the Peace Corps exhibited a generosity that I was sure had to be a characteristic of the country as a whole. I saw the eyes of children light up as a result of the clothes and food provided by America. I watched as the poor people of my region came to a building near my home to get milk, clothes, and food supplied by Americans. They would leave with their arms full and faces smiling. I wanted in on that. I wanted to be a part of it. Everything American seemed to be positive to me. These people came to my country and made every effort to make us feel good. They wore our clothes, learned our language, and enriched our lives. I couldn't wait to go and see this place they came from for myself.

So, I bided my time and was a dutiful daughter. I was very shy as a girl, but had this desire in me to be something more. I soon directed this energy into making my dream a reality. It started during high school with a job at The Cotton House. It was here that my interest in art began. At The Cotton House, African artisans were showcased and their carefully handcrafted artwork was sold to tourists. I spent my time observing and learning the retail trade.

The course of events that would change my life forever started there. One day after I had worked at The Cotton House for a few months, a Peace Corps volunteer came in and started a conversation with me. Melvin Foote was one of the few black men in the Peace Corps at the time and he showered me with attention. I was very embarrassed, but excited at the same time. To my surprise, he sent me flowers a few days later. I had no idea what to make of it. Then, as quickly as he had come into my life, he went away. My hopes were dashed and I tried to forget the handsome American.

A couple of weeks later, I went with a friend to a restaurant frequented by Americans. To my excitement, Melvin was there. I quickly pointed him out to my friend and told her I knew him. She didn't believe me, so I decided to prove it. In a moment of rare courage for this shy girl, I approached him to say hello. I wanted to prove my friend wrong and see what his reaction would be. There had been something about him, and I was disappointed that he hadn't come back for a visit. He encapsulated so much of what I hoped for and I wanted him in my life.

His face brightened when he saw me, and he not only bought my lunch that day, but he also asked me on a date. I was ecstatic! He had only been away on vacation! Of course, I wasn't allowed to date, so I had to be very creative in my way of getting around the rules. I surprised myself with my rebellion, but I was determined. I knew I had found a kindred spirit. We were immediately bound by our ambition.

My family had placed high expectations on their shy daughter. I always stayed within the rules and was supposed to marry the boy next door. They never expected me to leave or do anything other than what I was told. When I announced that I was getting married, their faces showed their shock and disappointment. They had always been accepting of the Americans in our community, but it was quite another thing for their young daughter to be marrying one. It wasn't in the plan.

Luckily, they eventually adjusted to the idea and gave us their blessing. I never wanted to sacrifice my family for my dreams, so I was very relieved when they accepted Melvin. We were married immediately and Melvin and I made a home for ourselves in Ethiopia. I continued to hope that America would be on the horizon one day, but I was patient. We moved to the city of Addis Ababa, where Melvin got a job teaching and coaching at the American School.

Our lives settled into a rhythm for a while and Melvin truly loved living in Ethiopia. The civil unrest around us was largely ignored for the time being and we soon found out we were expecting a child. We weren't planning to start a family right away, so the pregnancy was a surprise. While the suddenness of it put a strain on our relationship, Melvin expressed a strong desire for a son. After gaining my family's acceptance, I was determined to make it work. I didn't want to fail them or myself. So, I redirected myself into being a dedicated wife and expectant mother.

The upheaval and change in our lives was a reflection of the unrest in the country. Our emperor, Haile Selassie, was facing serious opposition. Under his reign, our country was suffering and he seemed to be completely focused on foreign affairs. By the early 70s, Ethiopia was gripped by a huge gap in the distribution of wealth, rural underdevelopment, government corruption, out-of-control inflation, unemployment, and a severe drought in the north. Meanwhile, our emperor was mediating disputes between other African nations and leaving us to fend for ourselves.

By February of 1974—around the time Melvin and I were married—frustrated workers, students, and soldiers began a series of strikes and demonstrations. In September of that year, Haile Selassie fell victim to a coup staged by members of the armed forces and was killed. A group known as the Derg was established to run the country with one of the coup leaders, Mengistu Haile Mariam, serving as chairman. By the next year, the monarchy was abolished and Ethiopia became a republic.

Mengistu soon started showing signs of wanting to consolidate his power. Several members of the Derg were killed in early 1977, reportedly on the orders of Mengistu. A group called the Ethiopian People's Revolutionary Party opposed Mengistu's actions and launched a campaign to undermine the military regime. This group was based in my province of Tigray and conducted urban guerrilla warfare against the regime. This came to be known as the "White Terror."

In response, the government provided arms to peasants, workers, public officials, and loyal students help the government's security forces root out their perceived enemies. This responsive campaign was called the "Red Terror," and, between the years of 1977 and 1978, approximately 100,000 people were killed or disappeared.

Relations between Ethiopia and the United States became strained over increasing human rights violations, ending a 20-year alliance between the two countries, in 1977. My family was miraculously spared during this whole series of events. I still do not know why. Most of the educated people we knew were either killed or fled the country during the "terrors."

It was a frightening time, and, by 1976, all Americans were asked to leave. Fearing for our lives, Melvin and I made the decision to leave as well. We had a son who was a year old and we were truly afraid. It was one of the hardest periods of my life. Even though I had dreamed of moving to the United States for so long, I hadn't pictured it happening the way it ultimately did. I was scared for my family and scared for myself and my son. Melvin didn't want to leave because he liked our life as it was. He became very frustrated by the turn his life had taken and our relationship suffered because of it. The illusion of a happy marriage was dissolving around us as we fled from my home to a new life and a fresh start in the United States.

Chapter 3

Survival Training

We will either find a way or make one.
—Hannibal

America. Land of the free and the brave. I was excited by the prospect of this new and strange world, but completely unprepared for what my new life would hold. After years of living in a nice home with household help, Melvin and I moved into a one-bedroom apartment in downtown Denver. For the first time in my life, I began to understand what it was like to be poor. Of course, poverty had touched me and moved me to tears many times over the course of my life in Ethiopia, but now it was me. I had no idea how we would make ends meet, how we would pay bills and feed and clothe our child. The stresses of the move and having no money were very hard on my marriage. It was now obvious to me that I would have to fight for the life I wanted and assumed would be afforded us in America.

So, I hit the pavement, so to speak. Within six months, I had a job at May D&F, an upscale department store, which is now called Foley's. I think I surprised Melvin with my determination. The timid girl that he knew from Ethiopia had suddenly become this strong woman with a plan. My dream to own my own business was ever-present in my mind as I took the job in the junior's department. I wanted to learn as much about retail in America as I could. Despite a bit of a language barrier, I immediately became a natural at selling and it felt good to be a success. I had always liked clothing and nice things, so this opportunity was a good fit for me.

We soon moved to a larger duplex east of Denver and things were okay for a while. My son was doing well in America, playing sports and making friends, and I tried to focus on him and not on the unraveling process of my marriage. So much had changed between Melvin and me. The whole dynamic of our relationship was truly based on our common love of Ethiopia, and this new life in America threw a wrench into all of those carefully laid plans. I wanted to make it work for the sake of my son and my family back home. It was too hard to admit I had made a mistake, but my life moved forward regardless, and I threw myself into my work.

Finally, Melvin made the decision for me. He moved out after one short year of living in America. And now I was alone with my son, Mengasha. For a time, I foolishly thought that I could stay married to Melvin and just live apart, but my desire to be independent kept nagging at me. I knew that I needed to be free—to be my own person at last. I needed to be 100 percent in control of my life and shape it for myself. I was so scared, yet, at the same time, I knew in my soul that I could do it. I *would* do it. Okay, so I was an immigrant from Ethiopia, I was now a single mother, I was in a strange country; but I spoke fairly good English, I had a good job, a place to live, and a burning desire to *be*. In retrospect, it scares me. I suppose you just do what you have to do in times like those—so we filed for divorce and I officially became my own person.

To keep it all in perspective, there was a war still going on at home. My family was in the middle of a true crisis, and, if they could make it through that, I knew I could make it in America. I worried about them daily and focused on building financial security for myself to keep my mind off of the danger they were in.

Soon, I was able to buy a house for Mengasha and myself. I was making very good money at the department store and had started making new merchandise suggestions to my friends who were buyers for the junior's department. Besides, I wanted Mengasha to have a yard and as regular a life as possible. He had lots of friends at school and was starting to show some promise as a basketball player. So, we bought the house, installed a basketball hoop in the driveway, and got back to the business of making a life for ourselves.

The house was in east Denver near the campus of Denver University. When I bought it, my friends were skeptical. It was old and in really bad shape. I guess my background with a father in construction gave me the ability to see past the obvious. I envisioned a beautiful showplace of a house that I would be proud of. And, it was all mine. So, despite the vote of no-confidence, I went to work. The house was gutted and redone. I had a garage built for the new car I had bought, and I planted a garden in the back yard. The American dream was becoming mine and I was high on life. I had done it!

I spent seven years working at May D&F, all the while learning about markup and sales decisions. I had record sales and was even named employee of the month several times over the years. I worked hard and I was rewarded with recognition and a good salary. It was a good time for me. I was meeting people, building my confidence, and learning all of the ins and outs of the retail trade. I was a good pupil and patiently plotted to institute a plan of my own.

I originally got the idea to sell African art from acquaintances who would come over to my new house. They were amazed by the work I had done on the place and were even more taken by the art I had brought with me from Africa. They showed a great deal of interest in several of the pieces, so I starting thinking that I could put a few things up for sale. I slowly added pieces to my collection and started to sell samples from my house. After a few years of moderate success at this home venture, I called my brother for advice.

My brother, Danny, has always been my idol. Through hard work and determination, he has made a solid name for himself in Ethiopia. He is now the most successful manufacturer of metal goods in the country. He had always been a very smart businessman and I patterned myself after him in so many ways. So, needless to say, I hung on his every word when I asked his advice about starting my own business venture.

I started by telling him that I had been selling art from Ethiopia from my house and wanted to open a store. I will never forget his words, "What is stopping you?" And he was right. Nothing was stopping me but myself. I had built up significant savings and knew what I needed to do. My brother encouraged me not to give up on my dream, and I was renewed. His words echoed in my head, "Tseghe, you can do it." I had made it this far and it was time to move ahead with my lifelong dream. I was going to make it happen.

I soon quit my job and enrolled in business classes at Denver Technical College. I wanted some education to complement my firsthand experience at the department store. I was afraid that there was some crucial piece of information on doing business in America that I was missing, and I really needed that extra boost of confidence to forge ahead. So education was my chosen path and I dove into it headfirst.

Once at school, I faced an entirely new set of hurdles. I felt self-conscious about my English and was terrified when an assignment forced me to speak in front of a group. To my amazement, I made good grades. A lot of the subject matter was very similar to my high school education in Ethiopia. There, high school had served as business school, so these classes were a refresher for me. I also added sales technique classes to my curriculum and quickly saw that my practical experience at May D&F had paid off.

I finished my schooling in two years and was ready to face the world. On to becoming the business owner I had always dreamed of—it was so close I could taste it.

Chapter 4

Round 1

To burn always with this gem-like flame, to maintain this ecstasy, is success in life.

—Walter Pater

Not long after I finished my classes, I read in the paper that the Tabor Center and Tivoli shopping centers were opening in downtown Denver. This was it! I thought one of these shining new places would be perfect for my African art boutique. I carried in my mind an image of how my store would look—modern, yet warm and welcoming—with a wide variety of the best African art I could find. I pictured my store as a centerpiece of one of these upscale shopping centers. It would be a gallery that would educate the entire region on the beauty of art from different African tribes and their culture. I knew the basics of making a store into a showplace; I had already achieved that with my own home. I could already hear the wineglasses clinking and the soft strains of jazz at my grand opening party. My brother Danny and other siblings would fly in especially for the occasion, and I would make them all so proud.

My first choice was the Tabor Center—it was in the heart of downtown and sure to bring in lots of shoppers. It had so much promise and was constantly in the headlines of the local dailies. *Tabor Center Mobbed . . . 25,000 mingle at speeches, balloons soar. Imaginative Tabor Center bucks age of safe thinking.* At that time in Denver's history (it was 1984), the downtown area was not very popular. People lived and shopped mostly on the outskirts in the suburbs, and downtown Denver was not the popular destination it has now become. These new shopping centers were going to change all of that and it felt like the perfect opportunity for me. I imagined myself in the forefront of the glamorous emergence of my new hometown. Timing was everything and now was the time! My hands were shaking as I reached for the phone to call the Tabor Center's management.

Within minutes, I knew my fate was not to be the Tabor Center—they were already full, completely rented. Okay. So. I had to shift that image a bit. Maybe I wouldn't be behind that great wall of glass facing 16th Street—the one I had seen renderings of in the newspapers. The one I had watched as it slowly emerged skyward from the turned up foundation of a multi-tiered parking garage.

Plan B. My store would be at the Tivoli! I could already see it! It was also a beautiful place that had lots of promise, so I went to them next. They still had space available. They gave me a tour and I was mesmerized by the opulence. It had been a brewery, built in 1859, and now $30 million had been spent to make the Tivoli a truly remarkable showplace. Crystal chandeliers hung from the three-story-high ceilings, the corridors between storefronts were vast and paved with marble, and the centerpiece was a fully glassed-in atrium that perfectly framed a magnificent view of the great Rocky Mountains. Newspapers across the country ran stories on its development and grand opening. They had produced brochures that were being sent around the world, and a five-star restaurant, the Rattlesnake Club, would soon be the draw for celebrity clientele visiting Denver. It oozed class and I decided on the spot that I wanted to be a part of it. As my visions of sugarplums drew me towards one of the gorgeous empty spaces near the heart of the complex, the management was ushering me to the back corner on the third floor. Undaunted, I opened my first store, Zebra Imports, in one of the worst locations in the Tivoli—but I was in the Tivoli and I had a store. The rest didn't really matter so much then.

I was soon swept up in the process of opening Zebra Imports. I followed all of the Tivoli's rules to the letter, even using their designer for the interior of my store. I became a picture-perfect tenant and didn't even complain when delays with the designer kept me from opening until 1986, nearly four months late. I traveled to Africa to buy inventory, carefully choosing special pieces. I wanted everything to be perfect.

My excitement was palpable. It almost seemed surreal to be opening an African Art store in America. My life had closed in on itself and now was opening up in full bloom. I imagined a caterpillar emerging from its cocoon; a tulip bursting upwards from the springtime soil. The scattered puzzle pieces of my life now had the last piece in place, and the resulting picture was beautiful.

I opened the doors to Zebra Imports in February 1986. We kicked off the opening with a party that was all I had dreamed of and more. About 50 family members and friends came to show me their support. It was one of those times in life when I can honestly say that I took pause to revel in the moment. Yes, I was already busy and caught up in the day-to-day activity of running a successful store, but I hadn't forgotten where I came from.

I thought back to my days at The Cotton House as I scanned my new, sparkling store. The artifacts of the skilled craftsmen from my homeland lined the walls and newly built fixtures. I could picture them working as I took in each piece. The potter with his hands covered in the gray dust of wet clay that dried as he worked. The woodcarver, his face scrunched in concentration as he perfected the nose of a mask made from locally cultivated mahogany. The sculptor silently chipping away at quartz recently mined from the mountains. Each piece had a story, the face of its creator behind it. That had been part of the draw for my customers when they came to my house. They would listen intently as I relayed the story behind the particular piece that had caught their eye. It wasn't a selling technique, it was just what felt right to me. The art was more than a dollar amount to be made. It *was* me. It was my way of bringing a part of my old life into my new one. And the merger was a successful one. I felt blessed. I had worked really hard to get here, but I knew from my father that hard work equaled success. That hard work had become the cornerstone of my life and subsequent achievements.

The business showed an almost immediate profit and a great response from the public. On one particularly memorable day, a woman came in to browse. I approached her and started a conversation. I soon learned that she was with the "Perry Mason" television show and they were interested in renting some art for the set of the show. It was incredible. I gave her some ideas and we picked out a few items. They not only used the art in various episodes, but Raymond Burr himself bought a few pieces for his personal collection. I felt that being in the Tivoli had helped my store gain visibility with these visiting glitterati. Regardless of my disappointment with my location, being in the Tivoli had given me the chance to share my passion for African art with a crowd I wouldn't have previously encountered.

The list of celebrities who shopped at Zebra Imports during those first years also included Jean Auel, author of *Clan of the Cave Bear.* It was such an adrenaline rush and gave me an increased faith in my choices in life. If high profile, successful people loved my art, then I knew I must be on the right track. It was the highest form of validation from my new country. If famous people—people highly regarded by American society—bought the art in my store, then I was onto something. With these people behind me, I knew that my store had what it took to last.

Everything was coming together nicely when a man came in who would, in many ways, change my life. He came in like a whirlwind—a dashing man with a million-dollar smile. He moved quickly—was high energy—and I was mesmerized by him. I watched him as he touched things, spinning through the room like a colorful top. Soon, he turned and faced me with a grin like a halo. He stuck out his hand to me and said, "I'm Don Hughston and I have an idea." Then he proceeded to lay out a plan for me. I could only nod in agreement as he breezed through his proposal. His idea was this: Franchise Zebra Imports—take it national. Reach thousands, millions with my inventory of art. He talked of catalog sales, finding investors—even using the Internet as a vehicle, and I didn't even know what the Internet was as it was only the late 80s. Nonetheless, I was seriously impressed and told him I would think it over. It was truly an intriguing proposition and one that really seemed to "fit." Franchising was the way American business people really became successful and Don Hughston had the knowledge to help make it happen for me.

Don Hughston's proposal struck a nerve for more reasons than the prosperity it promised. I had begun to hear rumors about a shift in the Tivoli's success. I knew that the city of Denver owned the property and had awarded the developers a 65-year lease that had a few caveats. Rumors had started circulating about the city taking the property back and giving it to the neighboring University of Colorado at Denver to use for classrooms and other academic needs. I kept telling myself that it was only gossip, and everything appeared to be business as usual. Still, it nagged at me and I felt this new direction would ensure my footing if I had to leave the Tivoli's opulent setting.

A couple of weeks later, the management of the Tivoli approached me about a new space. They told me that since I had fast become one of their premier tenants, they were rewarding me with a better location. They further explained that the uniqueness of my store was something they wanted to model the whole Tivoli shopping experience after and offered me a long-term lease. I immediately questioned them about the rumors I was hearing. "Should I worry about the rumors that you guys are going under?" I asked.

"No," they replied. "There is no way that we would have invested all of this time and money into a place and then just walk away."

I trusted that instinctively, and, inside, was soaring. I had faith that the Tivoli would be successful and put all of my focus on my business. This was truly incredible news and the timing was perfect. I had just signed off on a plan developed by Don Hughston that would make my friend and investor, Gloria Curtis, a full-time manager. The plan was a prototype for how the franchises would be run. I was now free to focus on building the business more, working with Don Hughston on the franchising deal, studying market trends and making long-term projections, and taking trips to Africa. It was a perfect arrangement for all of us. The new location was the icing on the cake. I gave the lease to my lawyer to review and signed it right before leaving for a buying trip to Africa. During the trip, I took extra care in picking art, keeping a picture of the new, expanded store in mind.

The new location was filled with light, and Gloria and I excitedly worked with the Tivoli's designer to create a perfect backdrop for the art I had chosen. Sales improved even more after the move and I really felt satisfied. Zebra Imports was my life now and I was finally doing what I loved. Despite the fact that the newspapers had started reporting the Tivoli's demise while I was in Africa, we had their word, so we focused on building Zebra Import's success.

After we settled into the more visible location, our reputation grew. The store continued to draw in visiting celebrities, as well as many of Denver's elite. I was in amazement at the life I now had. I had gone from a young impressionable girl in Ethiopia to a struggling salesperson at a department store, to being on a first-name basis with judges, celebrities, and the Denver elite. It really was incredible and I worked hard at not taking a bit of it for granted.

It was also very important to me to convey some of this to my son. I wanted his life to maintain its normalcy, but I wanted him to learn the same lessons I had learned from my father. That was part of the challenge of being single, a mother, and owning my own business. It was a constant battle to keep a balance. Melvin had since moved on to a career in Washington, D.C., and I was truly alone. No family nearby, just friends. So, it was up to me to make this work. Unfortunately, my newfound success took quite a different turn.

Despite my achievements in business, I began to realize that my 14 year old son needed more security than I could give him. Mengasha was at an age that required supervision and discipline, and I started to feel that I wasn't the one who could give him that. After some heavy-hearted discussions with Melvin, we decided that Mengasha would try living with his father in D.C. It was one of the saddest things I ever had to do, but I knew that it was best for him. I was home less and less and it wasn't fair to him. I had made it this far, but it had gotten bigger than me and I couldn't control it all any more. He ended up spending two years with his aunt in Chicago in a lively family with two other kids. He was really happy there and I knew it was good for him. In retrospect, the timing was fate. The events that followed would have been disastrous for Mengasha to witness.

With Mengasha gone, I decided to buy a condo downtown and rent out the little house I had lovingly renovated. I had been carefully plotting out my finances for some time, driven by my sometimes-irrational fear of going broke. This fear led me to be very careful with how I spent money. I was terrified of debt and refused to buy things with credit unless I knew exactly how long it would take me to pay it off. I tried to make smart decisions that might leave me a little strapped in the present, but would help build long-term financial security for me. Even in light of the success of my store, I couldn't just freely spend with no worries; it wasn't in my nature. With this steady discipline, I had been able to pay off my house, so the move to the condo made sense—especially since I was traveling a lot and Mengasha was home only for visits.

So, I moved into the condo and started a redecorating project that turned into another complete renovation. It was becoming a pattern with me. I would walk into a place—any place—and become my father in that instant. The walls of the structure would disappear as I envisioned wide-open spaces. By determining where the support walls were and tearing out the rest, I turned darkened corners into light-filled havens. It is still truly a passion for me. The process of making something into more—making a space beautiful and lasting—must have been genetically transferred to me from my father. This condo was no exception.

Business continued, I lived in the dust bowl that had become my apartment, and Mengasha came to visit as often as possible. Gloria and I tried to ignore the newspaper reports that were becoming more and more frequent. The *Denver Post* was reporting that the city was suing the Tivoli for breach of contract. Harder to ignore was the fact that tenants had started moving out en masse. We couldn't turn a blind eye any longer. It was obvious that the Tivoli's contract had been breached—they were required to maintain 75 percent occupancy, and, at the current rate of tenants leaving, it was only a matter of time. We decided it was time to start our search for a new location. It was the end of an era for us and Denver in a way—and it was a little sad. But it was business.

Gloria started the search for a new space close by and still downtown. It seemed like it would be an easy process because there were a lot of empty retail spots in the areas surrounding us. Denver was in a recession. The first place that looked promising was a retail development called Writer's Square. Gloria called the management, they came to see the store, and took a tour. The lease was literally on the table when they asked Gloria if she was the owner. She told them no and introduced me. I immediately sensed their hesitation. I guess they didn't expect the owner of Zebra Imports to be a black Ethiopian immigrant. The deal fell apart and we were on to the next potential property. It was such a painful process. We had a successful store that famous people patronized, yet no one in downtown Denver wanted to rent one of the many, many available spaces to us. I didn't understand it or expect it. I had a nice store with respected clientele—and it seemed as though the color of my skin was the only reason I couldn't get a decent rental space. I never expected the "land of opportunity" to have so many closed doors.

After an exhaustive search, we finally found a nice spot in Cherry Creek, an up-and-coming area in south Denver. It wasn't downtown, the location I thought best for business, but it was an area filled with art galleries, and we would really fit well there. My faith in humanity felt renewed at last. The store would live! Gloria and I made the decision to look forward as we made plans to move. Don Hughston was still working with us and had gathered some investors. So, as we were planning the big relocation to Cherry Creek, Don was working out another plan involving these investors to start the franchising arrangement. I felt the future was the best place to focus my energy—and not on the sting of so many rejections from the various properties in Denver. The future looked very bright for Zebra Imports and me again!

I turned my notice in to the Tivoli, and the brightness immediately dimmed. I felt that it was an open-and-shut deal since they were going under, they had lied about their situation when I signed the last lease, and my lawyer had even told me that I had to move out because their failure would destroy my business. But, it wasn't to be that way.

I was in the store with Gloria packing up when a man came in and handed me an envelope. "What is this?" I asked.

"The Tivoli is suing you for breach of contract," he replied, literally gazing down his nose at me, his tone filled with condescension. I quickly took in his tailored suit and crisp shirt. It screamed "corporate lawyer" back at me. I looked down at my own clothes and noticed they were covered in dust and newspaper print from the packing. I felt so small suddenly. Insignificant and powerless.

"What do you mean 'suing me'? For what? They are closing! I have to leave or I will lose my business!" The tears welled up in my eyes before I could stop them. This couldn't be happening!

"Have your lawyer contact me." And he turned and left.

I looked at Gloria and burst into tears. "Don't worry. We'll get this straightened out," she said over her shoulder as she ran to the phone to call our lawyer.

I wasn't so sure. My world had reversed itself and turned upside down, but in a bigger way than I could have ever envisioned. What were a few rejections from rental properties in the face of this? My worrying instinct told me that I could lose everything. I knew I had a case against them, but could I win it? I sunk to the floor as Gloria handed me the phone. "It's your attorney—tell him everything," she said.

We went to work immediately. With the help of my personal lawyer, I retained the best commercial law firm in Denver and sunk my heels in for a fight. We decided to countersue, and my outrage began to build. If there was one thing I knew how to do, it was fight back. I had struggled too long to lose it all. I pictured myself in front of a jury—wasn't that how the American justice system worked? I knew that a jury of my peers would understand my situation. That image, however, quickly vanished at the first hearing. There was a clause in the lease that stated I had waived my rights to a jury trial in any dispute with the Tivoli. It had seemed so unimportant at the time, and now here it was in black and white. There was my name on the line and I couldn't dispute that. It was to be a simple hearing and a single judge would decide my fate.

I spent the next months working with my lawyers to hire expert witnesses and to build a case against the Tivoli's developers. There was only one other tenant left in the building besides myself. It was ridiculous! Gloria took over most of the moving responsibilities while I focused on the case. I had to beat them or I feared I would lose everything.

It took a full year for the judge to hear our case. The day it was set, I went to meet my lawyer. He said that my legal team wasn't ready and that he wanted to file for a postponement. I trusted them implicitly—so I agreed. In retrospect, I thought it was odd that a year hadn't been enough time. I thought we were ready. But, I hadn't ever dealt with anything like this before, so I let him take the lead.

Later that morning, I went with my lawyer to the courthouse for our appointment, and we waited for the judge to call our case. I was shaking as we stood before him. The guy in the suit who had come to my store wouldn't look at me from his table. "Your honor, we are requesting a postponement to continue gathering evidence," my lawyer said as we stood.

The judge glared at us from his bench and said, "Motion denied. We will proceed with this case today."

I was shocked. I looked at this man I had trusted and he didn't look back at me. When he finally did look at me, he shrugged. No big deal. We can do this. My head was whirring—what about the witnesses we had hired? The evidence we had gathered? We didn't have any of that! How could we do this?

The next couple of hours were a blur. The Tivoli presented their case and called me to the stand. I couldn't stop crying. I was a wreck. I could barely answer the questions they posed. The judge continued to look down at me from his perch and I felt really afraid. "Ms. Foote? Did the Tivoli hold a gun to your head to sign this lease?" the judge asked at one point.

"No sir," I replied through sobs. Then, they started reviewing my financials. My house was paid for and I guess they thought it was my best asset. "It's worth $92,000," I heard someone say.

Then, it was over. The judge's booming voice pierced my brain, "I find in favor of the plaintiff, Hahn Company Developers. The defendant's countersuit is dismissed due to lack of evidence. Ms. Foote is ordered to pay $92,000 in compensatory damages."

The wind was knocked out of me like I had been punched. One swift blow to the gut. The judge didn't care about the big picture of the Tivoli's deception, the lies they had told me—all that mattered was that I had signed the lease. My assets were immediately frozen in lieu of the settlement. "We'll appeal, right?" I said as I attempted to compose myself and face my lawyer.

"Tseghe, I really don't recommend that. It will be expensive and not really worth it." He looked at me for a moment and said, "I have to go. I will call you later."

I watched his back as he made his way to the doors at the back of the courtroom. This couldn't be real, could it? I felt myself start to lose it again and let the tears wash over me in the now empty courtroom.

I was so glad that Mengasha wasn't living with me. Fate had obviously had a hand in that. It would have been so hard for him to see me in the state I was in. I wasn't sure if the tears would ever stop. I couldn't believe that the Tivoli could actually take my property—something I had put my own sweat and tears into. It was so wrong. As I handed over the key to my house a week later, I realized that I had just had my first boxing lesson. I had learned what it felt like to go up against a heavyweight and get knocked out of the ring. Round 1. Ding-ding!

Over the next few months, I dragged myself through the motions of setting up shop in Cherry Creek. The store was truly beautiful and my heart leapt as I walked through the doors one day after weeks of being in mourning. I had been so immersed in the lawsuit that I hadn't really paid a lot of attention to how it was all coming together. It was magnificent. Gloria was there, and so was Don, and they smiled as I came through the door. "Have I got some good news for you," Don said through a kilowatt smile. They sensed that I was back and were ready for me. The troubles slowly melted away as Don excitedly explained a trip he had planned for us and the investors. We were taking them to Africa to give them a firsthand tour of where the art in the store is created. They would meet the craftsmen and get a greater sense of the purpose. We decided to call this investment group The Guides—and make it a parent company to all of the potential franchises, including Zebra Imports. There was that future again. I was back and we left for Africa within two weeks.

The trip went really well and we decided that we were on the right track. I had also put together a proposal for Don and the investors on some potential charitable aspects of The Guides. We could use a portion of our profits to reinvest in the artists' communities—to build roads, schools. I was truly my father's daughter.

On the advice of friends, I had also retained a very brave lawyer who was willing to challenge the lawyers and the powerful firm that had failed me. He was an elderly man who was one of the few lawyers in Denver who wasn't afraid of this influential practice. He assured me that I had a case against them involving malpractice and he would take it. He retained an expert witness who could back up my claim, and simply wrote a letter to the law firm mentioning this witness' name. The letter asked for repayment of my lost assets. About a week after we sent over the letter, I had a check. I knew it! Round 2 and I was back in the ring!

I paid off my condo and was suddenly stronger. My survival instinct grew and was bolstered by this victory. I wasn't a victim anymore and wouldn't ever be again.

Business at Cherry Creek was good. For the two years I was in this location, we participated in the annual Cherry Creek Arts Festival held in July. This internationally acclaimed event drew thousands to the area and was very lucrative for us. We got lots of great exposure and our sales continued to climb. I had overcome some serious adversity and come out on top.

About a year after we made the move to Cherry Creek, the Tabor Center contacted me about renting a space. They were now anxiously searching for new tenants and began courting me with offers of new carpeting and customizing the store especially for me. They also offered to let me come into the mall on a month-to-month basis to try things out. That way, I had an easy out if the arrangement wasn't working. Since the Tabor Center was where I had always wanted to be, I jumped at the chance. I had enough inventory—as luck would have it—and they wanted me to move in immediately.

Two weeks later, Africa House opened on the third floor of the Tabor Center. It was the first time I had had two stores open at the same time, and it felt like a great move for The Guides. Another test-market opportunity. Don approved and so did the investors. It was a huge step for me and I started to think that this was truly what success felt like. The Tivoli had been glamorous—but now

I had two stores and a warehouse full of inventory. I felt the finger of fate tickling me and I was giddy with excitement. It had all worked out like it had for a reason.

The owners of the space we were renting in Cherry Creek decided to sell the property after we had been there for two years. They offered us the opportunity to buy the space, but we weren't ready for that. I had always felt that downtown was the location for me anyway, so—since we had the Tabor Center space—we declined and started making plans for yet another move.

I found a space on Wazee Street, a few blocks away from the Tabor Center in lower downtown. It opened as Africa House and was a gallery for designers, open by appointment only. It had been an auto repair shop and I thrived on the challenge of making it a showplace. It came together very nicely and was great advertisement because Wazee is a heavily trafficked street. People driving by would see the beautiful storefront and call to see my merchandise. It was a great arrangement and so much easier to manage than two actual stores. Gloria and I started spending our time and effort on building Africa House in the Tabor Center and managing calls from Wazee.

As our focus narrowed, I began to sense that Don and I were not on the same page anymore. He envisioned mass-produced African art and I knew that wasn't realistic. The pieces I sold were individually handcrafted and couldn't be produced any more quickly than they were. I also didn't want to sell anything that was of less quality, either. The investors had started to grow a little wary of Don, too. His ideas, while very creative, were too grandiose and not as rooted in reality. He saw an opportunity to make lots of money and I had started thinking more about the philanthropic aspects of the business. While I had welcomed his ideas to begin with, I now started to waver. I wanted to slow down and focus my energy. It had been eight years and it was time to bring the chapter to a close. The investors pulled out and Don moved on. I have lost contact with him now, but often think about what a great ride it was while it lasted.

At last, my life was becoming centered. I lived within walking distance from my store, Gloria was still helping me, Mengasha had moved back in with me and was in high school. Everything was flattening out and settling down. Africa House was doing well—extremely well. The Zebra Imports gallery was staying steady too. I decided it was time to take out a business loan and up the ante a bit. I wanted to really fix up the Tabor Center store and make it a permanent home.

I gathered all of my sales figures and financials and made an appointment with the bank. They quickly agreed to lend me $100,000 and I was on my way. The loan was secured by my condo, but it didn't concern me. I knew that I could pay it back within a couple of years with the current rate of sales from

Africa House. It was time to take the risk and really commit to this. I had a stable location and a clientele that had stuck with me through a recession. I had outlasted the Tivoli and maintained this customer base even as I relocated multiple times. It felt like I was finally where I needed to be, and I wanted to get the wheels in motion to secure this place.

I booked a trip to Africa and ordered several crates of inventory that I would store in my rented warehouse in Denver. I also hired a consultant to help me with long-term marketing and business planning. When I returned from Africa, I started inquiring about getting a long-term lease from the Tabor Center. I wanted them to know that I was here to stay. I was a good tenant, I always paid my rent on time or early, my sales were thriving, and the compliments continued to flow in about the store. People visiting Denver from out of state frequently came in and had things shipped to them at home. I felt accepted by the community at last. I had earned respect from customers and fellow tenants and was thrilled to be responsible for exposing the region to a whole new culture.

My inquiries for a new lease were put off temporarily because the Tabor Center was being taken over by new owners. They wanted to get the new owners in and have me work out a lease under their guidelines. It made sense to me. I had worked hard and they knew that, so it was only a matter of getting these new people to see my store and it would be sealed. I had no doubt of that. Besides, the Cherry Creek Shopping Center had become a viable threat to the Tabor Center's success by then. Some tenants had moved out, leaving quite a few vacancies, so they needed me.

Maybe I felt the rug under my feet shifting—but I thought *I* moved it as I walked forward—not that someone was tugging at the corner, trying to pull it out from under me. I had taken my gloves off and was heading out of the ring. The approaching opponent's shadow was behind me and invisible in my spotlight.

Chapter 5

Against the Ropes

Racism is easy to see, hard to prove, impossible to deny.

—Anonymous

The Yarmouth Group called a tenants' meeting to announce the addition and opening of the Cheesecake Factory about a year after they bought out the Tabor Center. They had mailed a letter to each of us with reassurances immediately after the purchase, but we hadn't heard much from them since they had officially taken over. This was in 1996. By this time, I had been with the Tabor Center for four years. I was ready to make the arrangement officially permanent. Now, the new owners I had been hearing about had arrived, and I went to the meeting smiling. I even tucked a pen in my day planner in expectation of the lease I would sign after the meeting. A couple of the other tenants and I walked down together and we were laughing at something someone said as we took our seats. As I sat down, I glanced around the table at the faces that had become so familiar to me. Even though we each had our own stuff to deal with as store owners, I felt a sense of community. We had grown to support each other over the years and I exchanged warm hellos as the owners of the various stores joined the group. Mike from the Hallmark store, Jana from Mountain Man Fruit and Nuts, Tom from the photography gallery. This was a group of people with a shared dream.

"Thank you all for coming today. I know how busy you all are," a stranger was addressing us, and I knew he must be one of the new owners. His suit was well tailored and expensive and his hair was freshly cut. Definitely corporate, I thought. He smiled and made eye contact with each of us as he introduced himself. "My name is Karl Erlich and I am a senior vice president with the Yarmouth Group. As you all know, we have been working towards buying the Tabor Center for about two years now. So, I have been preparing this speech for at least that long." He got a chuckle out of us over that and his smile deepened. Warming up the crowd. "The Yarmouth Group has been in the mall business for many years. So, we know a few things about running a successful mall. Under the leadership of my company, the Tabor Center is going to become a great place to have a store. We are confident that the plans we have in place will turn this mall around and attract customers and tenants alike. The bottom line for us is supporting your success, because if you are successful, we are successful—that's how it works." We all applauded, and I felt a little anxiety slide off my shoulders. This guy knew exactly what to say. The meeting went on for a while as he laid out marketing and renovation plans. Near the end of the meeting, he introduced our new property manager, Dan Hill. He stood only briefly and nodded at us in response to his introduction. I remember thinking how unassuming he seemed. I made a mental note: He was the guy to talk leases with.

It was getting late and the meeting finally ended. I gathered my stuff and looked around for Dan Hill. He was gone. I shrugged to myself and planned to make an appointment with him the next week.

Thursday came and I still hadn't gotten in to see Dan. I was closing up the store when Mike dropped by. "So, did you sign the lease yet?" he asked as he gave the metal gate that closes off the front of the store a little tug. It always stuck and I never could seem to get it to close all the way.

"What lease?" I asked, looking up from the register receipt I was reconciling.

"Dan Hill came by and offered me a long-term lease. He did the same with Jana. I just assumed. . . ."

"Well, I have been trying to get in to see him all week. I guess he has just been busy."

"Yeah. That's probably it. There are still a few of us and he has to make the rounds. It's probably no big deal."

“Yeah. I am sure that’s it. I’ll talk to him tomorrow. We’ll get everything straightened out. Thanks, Mike. Have a good night.”

“Good night, Tseghe. Do you need help closing up?”

“No, but thanks.”

I watched Mike’s back recede into the shadows of the mall and I felt a small knot re-tie itself in my stomach. Something didn’t feel right. My location on the third floor put my store right in the path of anyone heading to the food court. This Dan Hill had to have been by my store hundreds of times in the months since he had taken over, yet he had never once stopped in. I had never even known who he was before the tenants’ meeting. Now this. Everyone seemed to know him—to have met with him even—except me. Something was off kilter and I intended to find out what it was.

The next morning I left Kathy, a friend who sometimes helped me in the store, in charge and headed straight to Dan’s office. The receptionist, Paula, was there—she had been the receptionist under the previous owners too—I told her it was an emergency that I see Dan Hill. He was there and saw me right away.

“Good morning, Dan. I am Tseghe Foote, the owner of Africa House on the third floor.”

“Oh yes. Tseghe. Nice to meet you. Will you have a seat?”

“Sure.” I sat down across from him. Was that a nervous smile?

"What can I do for you today?"

"Well, Dan, I have been talking to some of the other tenants and discovered that you have been offering them long-term leases. I am wondering why I haven't been offered one as well."

He was definitely fidgeting now. He straightened some papers and avoided my eyes as he spoke. "Well. . . . I . . . we. . . . the reason we didn't come to you is because. . . . well, you just don't mix well." The words came out in a tumble. And I stared at him, my brain numbed at his words.

"What do you mean?" I would fix it. Make whatever it was right.

"Well, basically we need stores for the tourists and down-town workers." He now leveled his gaze at me and I felt myself slowly begin to unravel. Ding-ding went the bell in my head. Here we go.

"I bring in tourists all the time! I have a whole file of UPS receipts that show all of the places I have shipped things to for customers visiting from out of town! All over the country!" I couldn't conceal the panic in my voice.

He looked at me and I sensed alarm. I don't think he anticipated my file of receipts or my desperation or my strength for that matter. I can only assume that he expected me to withdraw quickly at his words and leave the office like a puppy with its tail between its legs. I had caught him off guard. "Okay, Tseghe. Why don't you tell me about your store. Give me the whole story."

I immediately launched into a brief historic overview—starting with my dream as a child in Africa up to the loan that I had just secured. I told him that I was projected to increase my sales three to four times each month. I was ready for him and I could tell that he wasn't ready for me. I had overwhelmed him with my details.

"Hmmm . . . ," he said as my story reached the present tense and I took a breath. "I have never been to your store. Why don't I come by to see it. I'll come by in a few minutes on my way to lunch." He pushed back from his desk and stood, signaling the end to our meeting.

"Okay, that would be great." I stood, too, and reached out to shake his hand. "See you in a few minutes then."

"Thanks, Tseghe."

True to his word, Dan Hill showed up at Africa House within ten minutes with his accountant in tow. I gave them the grand tour, explaining the art as I went and showing them specific tags on pieces to exhibit my attention to detail. The tags gave history on the pieces and a geographic perspective of Africa. They had become an established selling point and something that made the Africa House shopping experience unique.

"Wow," Dan said as the two men followed me through the store. "This place is like a museum."

I smiled at the compliment. I had won him over. "So what about that lease now?" I asked, feeling confident again.

"I don't handle long-term leases. Those are handled by Dee Torres who is based in Atlanta. I will call her right after lunch and ask her to call you to get a lease signed." He smiled brightly at me and shook my hand. "Great store," he said and headed out the door.

I almost jumped up and down in relief. I just wanted to stay there and use my loan to grow the business. I didn't want to deal with moving again and I liked it at the Tabor Center. I let myself relax—Dan Hill had seen that they were wrong about me not mixing well. I was a good tenant and I had shown him that. My place with these new owners felt secure again. What a relief.

About ten days went by and I still hadn't heard from Dee Torres. I didn't feel concern, though, because I knew she was busy and figured she might even wait to deal with my lease in person the next time she came to Denver. I hadn't been given any reason to think otherwise.

One morning a few days later, I came into my office at the store from the rear entrance. I almost always came in that way. I was looking for something in my purse as I walked in and almost ran right into a strange man in my office. I jumped back in alarm, and he looked startled too. I suddenly realized that my office furniture had been moved to the center of the room, my computer was unplugged and rested on the floor at my feet, and my phone teetered on the edge of my desk, its cord dangling limply to the floor. “Who are you? What are you doing here?” I practically screamed, my heart beating wildly in my chest. He just stared at me and didn’t answer. He clasped a clipboard tightly to his chest, almost like a shield. I was in shock. I brushed past him and headed out into the store calling for Kathy.

“Kathy! What is going on?! Who is this man in my office?!” Adrenaline was pumping through my veins from the fright.

“Mike brought him in this morning,” she said. I had known Mike Baca for the four years I had been at the Tabor Center. He was the head of maintenance.

“Mike?” I was still confused.

“Yes, Mike. He said the guy was taking measurements for insurance.”

“But I pay my own insurance.” I shook my head. My confusion would not recede. Then, as if on cue, Mike walked in. He took in the sight of Kathy and me in heated conversation. “Mike! What is going on here? There is a strange man in my office moving stuff around and he almost gave me a heart attack when I came in just now!”

“Don’t worry! He is here because of insurance. The new owners want to re-appraise the property to try to get a lower premium.” Mike smiled at me reassuringly.

“What insurance, Mike? The tenants pay their own insurance. It has been that way forever.”

“It’s for the whole shopping mall.”

"Then why didn't I receive a memo? You guys always do memos to let us know when stuff like this is happening."

"I know and I'm sorry about that. He just showed up today so there wasn't time. I'm sorry for the inconvenience, but he'll be finished soon." He gave me a quick pat on the arm and left the store.

Mike was an honest person and I believed him. We went back a few years and he had helped me out more times than I could count, so I took a couple of deep breaths and smiled at Kathy. "I guess it's okay then."

She shrugged and we got on with the day.

Hours passed and the guy was still in my store. Despite Mike's reassurances, I kept thinking that it still didn't quite add up. The tenants were required to carry up to a million dollars in insurance for the inside of the store. Why would the mall need someone to take measurements *inside* my store? This guy was in the store all day, using a ladder, removing ceiling tiles. My customers were having trouble getting around and I grew more and more irritated. Everything was chaos and he wasn't cleaning up as he worked. Finally, I approached him. It had been five hours at this point. "Gee, if it is taking you this long for just my store, it is going to take you forever to measure all of the other stores too!!!"

"What other stores?" He looked at me blankly.

"Well, the other stores in the Tabor Center. I thought you were doing the whole mall."

"No! I was only sent to do your store."

"I thought you were measuring for insurance for the whole mall." The confusion was back.

"Oh no. I am a subcontractor and was hired to do this store only. I'm not with an insurance company, ma'am." He seemed amused by my confusion and falsely reached conclusions.

My expression fell and betrayed me. My hands and lips started to tremble with anger. Who was telling the truth here?! I spun away from him without another word and walked directly to the phone. I was calling Dan Hill right now! He had some answering to do. As soon as I heard Dan's voice, I skipped the pleasantries and went straight for the jugular. "Dan! What is going on?! I have had a man in my store for the past five hours moving my stuff, distracting customers and generally wreaking havoc. Mike says he is with the insurance company, but now the guy says he isn't. What in the hell is going on here?" I was seeing red. I had had it!

"Let me talk to him, Tseghe." His voice was even, unruffled by my fury.

I called to the guy and handed him the phone. I could only hear his end of the conversation. "I am almost finished," he said into the phone. Then, he handed the phone back to me, eyeing me cautiously. I must have had steam pouring from my ears.

Dan's voice almost seemed distant. "Okay, Tseghe. He is with the insurance company. Sorry for the confusion. I promise you it will not happen again. He is almost done and he will be out of your hair. I appreciate your patience." He was speaking in that “don’t worry” tone I had heard before. I let him finish and then hung up.

It still didn’t seem right. Why would this guy, who was an outsider, lie to me? He had no reason to. My gut—which was knotted again—told me Dan was lying this time. The only thing I could think of to do was to call my lawyer. He could figure out a way to get everything in writing—get the pieces to fit together. I kept hearing Dan’s voice saying, “You don’t mix well.” Then, “He’s with the insurance company.” Mike’s face appeared, then Dan’s and Mike’s faces mixed together and the phrases switched. I grabbed the phone. My lawyer would get to the truth.

I got him—Phil Pankoff—on the line and explained the story to him. He agreed to call Dan and call me back.

It took Phil a day or so to reach Dan and call me back. I was beside myself by then. I had played out every possible scenario and all of the worst ones kept coming back into view. When the phone finally rang, and it was Phil, my heart started to race. “Tseghe, I have bad news for you. The guy in your store was taking measurements for a new tenant. The Tabor Center has rented your space to GNC.”

“What? What are you talking about ‘rented my space’?”

“Dan Hill said that they have rented your space to GNC and the guy that was there was taking measurements for GNC so that they can begin renovation plans. Mr. Hill says that Dee Torres will be calling to talk to you about options.”

“How can they do this, Phil? Why wouldn’t they have told me by now? I don’t understand why they would do this to me!”

“I don’t know, Tseghe. That’s all Dan Hill said. See what this Dee Torres has to say and call me back.”

I slumped down in my chair in my newly rearranged office. I could feel the tears starting and I struggled to keep them away. How could a mall that was 65 percent vacant be evicting me? This just didn’t register as being right. In fact, it was wrong. I decided to wait to see what Dee Torres had to say before I did anything else. I didn’t have a choice. I had this loan secured with my house, and the crucial Christmas season was a couple of months away. I couldn’t move again and survive it this close to Christmas. Dee had to have a solution for me—I was a good tenant! I had done everything by the book!

The call from Dee Torres came the next day. I was in my office and Kathy was managing the store out front. As soon as I heard her voice, I started to cry. I couldn’t control it. I had so much to lose and I felt so helpless. “How can you this to me? I have been a good tenant all of these years and now this? You guys don’t even warn me? Nothing? I am a single woman! I just took out a loan for my business and I could lose my house! Why didn’t you tell me this?”

Her voice was filled with venom. “Ms. Foote, you didn’t sell $800,000 last year and I don’t deal with people who sell less than that.”

"I am in a 1,000-square-foot space! Who sells that in a space this small?!" I cried. I was outraged.

"GNC does." Nothing more, nothing less. Just that. No kindness, just the bottom line for me. I was completely emotional, pouring out my heart to this woman, pleading to her female side—Please have some compassion for me! I thought she would get that.

"Not here! GNC was here before and failed. They went out of business!" It was the truth. It had happened in 1990. I knew because I had been a customer.

"Now, I know that isn't true," she said, condescendingly. But I knew it was. And I couldn't stop crying. It was so unbelievable. After all that I had been through up to this point and now here we were. Two voices across a phone line—and my dream was ending. Just like that. They were doing this to me—TO ME. It felt completely personal—"You don't mix well." Then the cover up and deception. My tears were endless and coming from a place so deep within me that I didn't even know it was there. She abruptly changed her tone, hoping to quell my rising hysteria. "It's going to be okay," she said. "Are you okay?" she interjected. Then, I took the bait when she asked, "How long have you been in business? Tell me your story." My sobs abated as I told her everything. I thought I had gotten through to her and that my story would break through a wall, appeal to her as a fellow businesswoman.

As my story ended, a hopefulness crept into my tone. And it abruptly exited. "Well, I am sorry, but there is nothing we can do for you, Ms. Foote. I may be able to find a space for you for a couple of months, but then you will have to leave. The bottom line is that your sales aren't good enough for the shopping mall. So, I will have Dan call you about a place for the short term. Good luck." And that was it. I was out of the Tabor Center. Just when I thought I had a foothold, the ground shifted again beneath my feet.

Within a day, Dan Hill called me. I bristled at the sound of his voice. I pictured his rumpled suit and the hands straightening papers as he spoke. "Tseghe, listen, I know you're upset—"

"Upset?! Of course I'm upset!" These people had some nerve!

"Wait! Listen to me a minute! I want to try to help! I think I may be able to find you a place downstairs—the guy in 202 may move out in November. Let me talk to the landlords and see if you can move there for one year. It will at least give you time to sell your inventory and save your house. What do you think?"

"Well, at least it's something. Better than my other option—which is closing." So, Dan had a little heart after all. "Thank you."

I was still hesitant to let my guard down. I knew I would never trust any of them again. I felt like I was in the first car on a rollercoaster: the spiral downward, followed immediately by a quick jerk up again. The only thing was, I couldn't see around the next bend and was forced to let the ride take me where it would.

A day or so later, it was Dan again on the phone. He said there was a problem and he needed me to come to his office. Okay. So, now what? Forget the rollercoaster—this was fast becoming a boxing match. They threw a punch, I ducked. I braced and brought my gloves up to my face—where was the next punch coming from? I was ready. So, I headed down to Dan's office with my gloves on.

There was the suit, the guy, and the hands—just like I knew they would be. At least some things were predictable. He smiled at me as I walked into his domain. "Close the door, will you?" Not a good sign. I tightened the laces on my gloves as I took the seat across from him.

"So, here's the deal. I don't have a space for you."

"Why? There are so many vacant stores! How can there not be a space?"

"Well, I am going to tell you a story that may help explain things." There was that bell again. I tried to think of what round we were on. Tried to figure up how many rounds I had left in me. "When the Yarmouth Group executives first came to tour the Tabor Center last year, they decided which tenants could stay. When they got to Africa House, they pointed and said, 'This has to go.'"

"What? What has to go? What's wrong with Africa House?" My brain struggled to decipher what he possibly could mean. I had a strong reputation and fine, quality art—even Dan himself had said that.

"I don't really know how to say this, Tseghe. They just said it isn't glamorous enough." His eyes were studying his hands like he had never noticed they were attached to his arms.

"I don't understand, Dan. What can I do?" I was in complete denial. Every fiber in my being wound itself up tight and screamed "NO!" This was not happening. This just did not happen in America.

"They feel it devalues the property and we have to add value to get new tenants and customers. Having a store like yours devalues the whole mall." His lips were pressed together in a tight line. His hands were clenched together on the desktop. His eyes looked everywhere but directly into mine.

"I can change the name—the name doesn't matter that much anyway. And the sign—we can make a new one that looks even nicer. I don't want to lose my store. I'll do anything they want. That's what they meant, right? The sign? The name? Is that the problem?" Let it be, my mind prayed. Please, let that be it.

"No. It's just the whole thing."

A silence filled the room and replaced the oxygen. I couldn't breathe. This punch had left me pinned against the ropes. It was "the whole thing." No hidden meanings there. It was me, it was the art, it was

Africa. Not glamorous enough for the Tabor Center. Could this all really be happening simply because I was from Ethiopia, selling African art? In Denver, Colorado, at the end of the twentieth century, could prejudice this blatant still truly exist?

"Once GNC signs, you'll be getting your eviction notice." The sound of his voice broke the silence and made me jump. "You should go ahead and start to pack up because all we need is that signature and you are out. We wanted the spot occupied up until they were ready, and now they are ready." The words sounded especially harsh and it was with obvious effort that he delivered them sternly.

I don't remember saying anything else to him or even walking back to my store. I delivered the news to Kathy like I was in a trance. She was incredulous. "Are you kidding me?" she asked with her brow furrowed.

"No, it's over," I said and turned away from her gaze. I needed to be alone. I wanted to go home and crawl in bed and never emerge again.

By the next day, I felt I had cried myself out. I had to do something to save all that I had worked for. I couldn't let them beat me. I had spent my entire life building this dream and I couldn't, and wouldn't, give up that easily. So, I pulled myself out of bed and started making calls to some real estate brokers I knew. I called two, Pat McHenry and Stuart Schwartz. I explained my story and impressed the urgency of my situation upon them. Something along the lines of, "I could lose everything if I don't find a place before Christmas." They got the picture.

Pat knew me and shopped at my store. I told her that I really needed to stay somewhere close by in order to maintain as many customers as possible. I explained that I wanted to have two people looking for me to speed up the process. Whoever found a space for me first would win, in essence. She promised to do her best. She even knew the owners of Writer's Square personally.

Stuart Schwartz was located in the Tabor Center. When I called him, he was surprised. He asked me why I was looking when the Tabor Center was so empty. After I filled in the details for him, I told him that I was a little concerned that I would have the same problem with another location. If I wasn't good enough for the Tabor Center, what would keep other properties from feeling the same way? So, he decided to come down and take a look at my store. He wanted to get a feel for my merchandise so that he could more effectively sell my store to a new landlord.

I met him at the Food Court adjacent to Africa House and we talked for a few moments before heading into the store. Standing in front of my store with a guy I hadn't seen before was Dan Hill. They were talking and pointing at the Africa House sign. Stuart and I walked past him without acknowledgment and I proceeded to give Stuart a tour. I continued to keep an eye on Dan as we walked through the store and reviewed the products. Finally, my curiosity got the best of me. "Excuse me for a minute, Stuart," I said and headed back out towards Dan. "Dan! What are you doing here? What do you want?" I was tired, completely exhausted, and not in the mood to dodge any more punches.

"Well, the guy downstairs in 202 may be moving after all, so we are talking about getting you a small sign for that location. If he does move, you can have that spot for two months, so we want to have a sign ready." He looked at me expectantly.

I wanted to deliver the punch this time. Knock him flat. "Dan, I have already told you that I need a permanent location. I am not some fly-by-night store. Besides, that guy in 202 doesn't even know what he is doing yet!" I took a deep breath and a step closer. My finger poked the air in front of his nose. "You kicked me out! I didn't do a thing wrong and you kicked me out! Now, I have hired Mr. Schwartz to find me another space so that I don't lose my business and my home. Is that clear enough for you?" By the time I finished speaking, Dan had taken a step back. His face was red and there was a single droplet of sweat on his brow. I didn't realize it, but Stuart Schwartz had come to stand behind me during the exchange.

Dan spoke directly to him over my shoulder. "Uh, why don't you guys come to my office and we can talk."

"Sure," Stuart said, still standing slightly behind me.

"Does three o'clock work?" Dan asked, finally speaking directly to me.

"Yeah—Stuart?" I turned to him and he winked at me.

"We'll be there."

The minute Dan was out of earshot, Stuart said, "Wouldn't that be great? If you could just stay here?" I couldn't help feeling a little hopeful, in spite of myself. Maybe they understood that I meant business, that I was a serious businesswoman after all.

"Sure, Stuart. That would be great."

We arrived at Dan's office promptly at three. This was becoming a ritual of sorts: I walk into Dan's office, Dan smiles at me, I take a seat, Dan starts to fidget, I wait for the first uppercut to be thrown.

As soon as we got in the door, Dan said, "This is wrong." Stuart and I just looked at him. "I am first to admit that what we are doing to this lady is wrong." I sucked in a breath that made a little whooshing sound. Oh, boy. Where was this heading? "You know, we come to this mall and think we know everything, but we don't. And what we are doing here is wrong."

"Thank you, Dan. This really shows leadership. You made a mistake and you are able to admit that. That really shows leadership." The relief I felt was immense. It oozed from every pore. Yes, what they had done to me was horrible, but they were going to make it right now. I smiled at Dan, and Stuart and I took our seats.

"So, let's fix the problem then," Stuart said. "If you are willing to admit that what you are doing is destroying her, then let's fix it. Let's sign a lease and keep her here."

"Stuart, you know why we can't do that."

"No, I don't. Why not?" Stuart fired back.

"We don't have a space. GNC has rented her space and they will be signing the lease any moment. There is no place for her."

"What about 202?" Stuart was ready for him and I just let him handle it.

"The guy hasn't decided for sure if he is leaving, and, if he does, that space is spoken for. She can have it for two months, but no longer."

In answer to this, Stuart produced a blueprint from his briefcase. He deftly spread it out across Dan's desk and walked around to stand beside Dan so they would be viewing it at the same angle. I wondered what Dan would do with his hands now that his papers were covered. But, as Stuart started pointing out other vacancies to Dan, my eyes darted to the spot marked 322—Africa House. I had already been removed from the blueprint—it was if I had never existed. I had already disappeared into thin air. I took in another breath.

"What about this one?" Stuart asked, pointing to a vacancy on the second floor.

"That is spoken for already."

"Okay. What about this one?" This time it was a first-floor spot.

"Oh. That one is going to be expanded into one large store."

Stuart shook his head. "Wow. You guys must be doing really well if you have leased all of these spaces already."

Dan stared at him. He almost looked angry. "You know, why don't I get Dee Torres to join us on the speaker phone so we can go over this with her." He dialed the numbers, mumbled something into the phone, and then placed the receiver in the cradle. "Dee? I have Stuart Schwartz and Tseghe Foote here. Ms. Foote really would like to stay here and Mr. Schwartz is helping her with securing a lease."

"Well, her sales aren't good enough for a long-term lease," Dee said, the irritation in her voice palpable.

"Actually," Dan said, pulling out a file and opening it. "I have her figures right here and her sales have been going up." There was a split second of silence from the speaker.

"Have you talked to her about changing the name?" I looked up at Dan as I waited for his response.

"Yes, we have talked about that a lot," Dan replied anxiously.

"Yeah, we sure have," Stuart added. "We have agreed to make it any name you guys want." We looked at the speaker, as if it would spontaneously combust. It was quiet. "So, Dee, what about the space on the end of the second floor?" Stuart asked.

"That one is spoken for." Her voice was flat.

"Wow! I was telling Dan that you guys must be doing really well since you have all of these places leased already. You must be excited." Stuart's voice was edged in sarcasm.

"Yes, we are. Actually, we are completely full."

I waited for something to happen. A space someone had overlooked to jump up off of the page. Instead, Dee Torres bid us good-bye, and I still had no lease. As we were leaving the office, Dan said, "I will keep you posted about 202. I can't promise anything, but it will buy you two months at least."

As Stuart and I headed back down the hall, he tapped me on the arm with the rolled up blueprint. "You don't even exist," he said, with a sideways grin. "You are operating your business illegally because on the blueprint you are gone. What do you think of that?" It was so preposterous that I couldn't help but laugh. I still existed in the mall and even had customers in the store as we headed in, but on the blueprint I had been completely erased. It was kind of funny in a twisted sort of way, like an episode of the "Twilight Zone" or something.

I decided then that I had only had two options. I would wait to hear back from Pat and/or Stuart about a new space and keep my fingers crossed that GNC would decide not to sign that contract. As long as I didn't have an eviction notice, I felt that I had a chance at keeping my current spot. So, until that happened, I would run my invisible business as always and hope for the best. If I could at least hold them off until after Christmas, I had a chance at salvaging everything.

The results of the rental property search were not good. Even Pat's personal contact refused me and Africa House. I was running out of options quickly. There was no way for me to pay off that loan without selling my inventory first. Now, I just had to hope that I wouldn't get an eviction notice.

October 14, it came. They delivered it to the store and sent a certified copy to my house. It was officially over and my options had run out. The search for another space had come up empty with both brokers and now I held an eviction notice in my hand. I looked around the store at the shelves filled with art from the people of Africa. I was surrounded by the dreams of so many people—artists who made a meager living creating items of beauty to sell. My dream of introducing that beauty to others was starting to fade, like an old photograph that starts to blur and brown around the edges. Maybe it had never been mine to begin with. Beauty is an elusive thing and maybe I had never really owned it at all. Tears began to stream down my face as a sob erupted deep from within. I slid to the floor and didn't notice the stains my tears made on the paper I still clutched in my hand.

Chapter 6

Serious Contender

If you lose hope, somehow you lose the vitality that keeps life moving, you lose that courage to be, that quality that helps you to go on in spite of it all.
—Martin Luther King, Jr.

As I unlocked the door, the phone was ringing. I dropped my bag on the floor and rushed over to grab it. As I picked up the receiver, I looked back and noticed an envelope on the floor by the door. A special delivery, no doubt. Another eviction notice, in case I hadn't received the other two copies already. This one was in a certified mail envelope.

"Hello?" I said into the receiver, my full attention still on the envelope I couldn't reach.

"Tseghe? It's Norma." Norma. A flood of relief washed over me as the feeling of calm her voice always brought registered. As quickly as it came, the calm retracted—a wave hitting the sand, then pulling back with the tide. I immediately started to cry and felt like I always did when I heard my mother's voice and I was upset. I knew she knew. Whatever it was, she would know instinctively. Norma was the same way. I had known Norma Paige for three years. We met when I was thinking of converting my showroom into a cultural/educational complex for the community. She had experience in marketing and public relations and was referred to me by a mutual friend. We instantly connected on so many levels—emotionally, creatively, spiritually—and became fast friends. Her friendship had always been free of judgment. Was true and real. "Are you okay?" she asked, her voice filling with concern. I had talked to her earlier in the day, right after the messenger had arrived with the first notice.

"No. Yes. No." I wanted to be. I wasn't.

"Okay, listen. I have been thinking about this thing and they just cannot do this to you. CAN–NOT." Her voice was strong, assured. I felt the strength surge and flow into my ear through the phone line.

"I know," I said, vainly attempting to control the leakage from my eyes. "But what can I do? It's done. Africa House is out of the Tabor Center. You can't get much clearer than an eviction notice. The timing is just . . . it's just awful . . . right here before Christmas. I have no choice but to close." I grabbed a paper towel and mopped my tear-stained face.

"No. You do have a choice. The Civil Rights Commission." The conversation paused as her words sunk in. "I called an attorney friend and he said he thinks you have a case. He recommends filing with them immediately. You have to go right now if you want to stop this eviction."

My mind was reeling and my legs threatened to betray me, so I sat down. I was shaking. "I can't go anywhere. I have been crying all day. I swear, I think I am losing it. They will think I am some crazy woman!" I couldn't imagine even standing up at this point, much less mustering the strength to walk into the Civil Rights Commission! Why was this happening to me?

"Tseghe, pull yourself together. I will meet you there. Here is the address." She hung up and I sat there with the receiver in my hand, the dial tone cutting the silent air.

Okay. I could do this. I had to. I blew my nose into the paper towel and tossed it into the trash. I stood and faced the mirror in the foyer. "You can do this," I said to the reflection. The face of a young girl looked back at me. The very face of the girl who had spent her youthful days in Ethiopia watching artists sculpt and create—while her own dreams took shape and grew. No, I couldn't just give up now.

When Norma and I reached the Colorado Civil Rights Commission office, we were ushered into a darkly paneled room filled with books. Titles leapt off the spines at me: *The Abolitionist Legacy, The Age of Rights, The Autobiography of Malcolm X.* Fifteen minutes later, a woman about my age came into the room. She talked quickly as if she could sense my urgency. "You must be Tseghe. We spoke earlier." She smiled and shook my hand. She pronounced my name "Teesiggie" and I made no move to correct her as I clasped her hand. She smiled at Norma in greeting and we took our seats. "So, Tseghe, you explained the gist of the situation to me on the phone. And I do understand that we need to move as quickly as possible. What I have done is put together the basic paperwork needed to file with us." She showed us the paperwork and gave a brief description of the minimum requirements. "However, given the urgency of the situation, I would highly recommend that you contact an attorney aside from us who is experienced in civil rights litigation." She passed me a card. "This is the guy. I'm not really supposed to make referrals, but he is someone I trust." She smiled at me again. And I nodded to her and glanced down at the card. We finished filing the paperwork to set the wheels in motion, said good-bye, and I dragged myself home.

The next morning I went to Africa House. From my office there, I called the number on the card from the lady at the Civil Rights Commission. David Fine. Luckily, he was in his office and listened intently as I gave him the synopsis. He said he would come over that afternoon. It was happening. There was no turning back now. The Tabor Center was in for a fight.

David arrived and we called Stuart Schwartz since he was an actual witness for me now. Stuart came right away and met us at the food court and told David all that he knew, not missing a detail of what Dan Hill and Dee Torres had said to me in the meeting. David took copious notes, his mouth in a grim line as Stuart spoke. He interrupted only to ask questions, nailing down every detail. We spent about an hour together, and by then it was close to five o'clock. I was exhausted from the day and the quick succession of events. The meeting concluded and we all shook hands. "Looks like we are ready, Tseghe," David said, turning to me as he closed his folder.

"Ready? Is there something we can do?" I wasn't sure of my legal footing yet.

"Yes. I am going to file an injunction in federal court to block the eviction first thing in the morning. It will be quicker than the Civil Rights Commission—they can take a while. I'm going to go to my office now to draw it up." He smiled at me and patted my shoulder. "We'll get 'em. Don't you worry." He shook Stuart's hand and left. I thanked Stuart for his time as he headed back to his office. I began to feel the first flicker of hope.

David filed the injunction the next morning as promised. The judge assigned to the case called a hearing and set it for first thing the following day. He would decide if I could stay or if I had to move out while I proved my case against the Tabor Center.

The Tabor Center attorneys called David to work out a compromise by mid-morning. The tenant in 202 had decided to leave and they gave us the option of moving there until the court case was settled. We knew that if the judge ruled for me to stay in my current location, the Tabor Center would be in a huge mess with GNC and could possibly try to hold me liable for the repercussions if my case was dismissed. GNC would be looking to recoup damages for lost business and breach of contract from the Tabor Center, who, in turn, would consider me the cause. The complications and potential for legal ramifications were endless and it scared me. I had everything to lose.

By 10p.m. we reached an agreement. Africa House's new, but temporary, address would be 202. So, the fight to not be thrown out of the mall entirely would continue, but from a new headquarters. I felt safer taking this option because I still wasn't confident that my case wouldn't be thrown out, and getting sued by both the Tabor Center and GNC, two huge corporations, was not something I wanted. We all agreed that it was the best option for everyone, with the least risk. The new space wasn't as prominently located as my third-floor spot by the food court. It also had an additional 1,000 square feet that would have to be filled with merchandise and displays. But, I wouldn't have to close my doors before Christmas. I had a place to go. And, I would have time to work at paying off the loan and save my house.

After we reached this compromise, David and I parted ways. He had saved my business and I owed him so much. His firm, however, was realistic about the potential for the case to drag on and they warned me that it would take a lot of time and money to fight. They were afraid that it just might not be worth it in the long run. I knew that what they were saying was probably right and that I might be crazy for not listening to them. But, this was more than a case to me already, and no matter how tired or frustrated I was, I knew that I hadn't done anything wrong. I knew that the Tabor Center had simply evicted me due to prejudice. And, I knew that I didn't want it to happen to anyone else. So, with a heavy heart, I decided to proceed without David. I think he understood, but it was sad. He had acted quickly and efficiently and I owed him everything for that. I just knew that I had to have a law firm behind me that truly believed in my case and was willing to stick with me through the bitter end.

I ended up taking a friend's recommendation and calling Darold Kilmer and David Miller. They had a long list of experience in civil rights cases and I was very relieved when they decided to take mine.

So, I moved at the end of October, 1996. I was able to re-open in ten days thanks to the Wazee Street showroom. The owners were selling the building, so I moved out and was able to fill up the additional 1,000 square feet in the new space at the Tabor Center. The timing actually worked out perfectly. Now, I could focus my energy on selling my inventory, paying off the loan, and waiting for a trial. It was the hardest wait of my life.

It's hard to describe, but I felt as if my whole existence was in a holding pattern. My fate was held in the hands of a person whom I had never met—another judge who would decide my life from his perch. Although I knew that the trial was at least a year away, the judge could dismiss my case at any time if he suddenly decided there wasn't probable cause. It was difficult, at best, to not think of that every time the phone rang—so my anxiety was high. If the case was dismissed, it would trigger a chain of events that were being held together now by only a thin thread of hope. The series would start with my being officially out of the mall, which would then mean that I would have to close Africa House. As soon as the store closed, I would owe a balloon payment on the loan I had secured. Since I would still be holding inventory, I wouldn't have the freed capital to make that payment. Since the loan was secured by my home, the bank's recourse to my nonpayment would be to seize my property. I pictured it like a fuse on a stick of dynamite—the case dismissal lighting the fuse, leading up to the explosion of my dreams and my life.

I spent every waking moment pondering the dynamite and waiting for the explosion. Twenty years of work could be flushed down the drain with one phone call. I was unraveling from inside out, in a slow, painful progression. The tears would start and a cherished customer would be left standing at the register with no one to pay. My mind would already be racing—am I going to lose everything?

Will I be homeless? How much longer was it all going to go on? The customer service I had always made a priority was suffering as I suffered. The business I had cultivated since I was 14 years old still had to be run, but I couldn't concentrate. There was no escape as I awaited my fate. You can't escape from your own mind.

A month after I moved to number 202, I got an unexpected phone call. A reporter from *Westword,* an independent newspaper in Denver, had picked up my story from court documents. As he interviewed me, I began to realize for the first time what I was in the middle of and my perspective shifted. I wasn't just a single mother, an African immigrant, or a black woman—I was a voice for all three. A voice that was speaking loudly about what was right and what was wrong in the world. As I answered his questions, my sense of purpose strengthened momentarily and I felt justified and empowered. I was going to make a difference for more than just myself. I was going to start a process that would help make sure that this never, ever happened to anyone ever again.

The story ran a couple of days later and the Tabor Center was quoted as denying it all. They called my allegations "false" and "outrageous." It was the first story in a series that *Westword* ran. It wasn't long before other news organizations picked up on it and I was besieged with calls. I patiently handled every interview, clearly understanding now that this was much bigger than me and my story. As the stories were printed, I started gathering clippings that I framed and displayed in my store. Customers who came in would almost always stop to read the articles. They always had a kind word and a question to ask. It was exhausting at times, but I knew it was necessary. People had to know that this was happening in their midst, that it still went on in the present tense. Prejudice was not dead—it was alive and well, thank you. And, it didn't have to be. There was something that could be done to stop it if you were up for the fight.

The first hint towards resolution came in the form of a settlement attempt by the Tabor Center in February, 1997. They were offering me yet another space within the Tabor Center for a year, and only a year. After the year was up, according to the settlement, I was to move out permanently. They were missing the point and I wanted them to know that. I wasn't interested in money. I wanted them to admit they were wrong—publicly.

By May of 1997, the trial had been set for January of 1998—one year and four months after the whole saga had begun. I still hadn't heard from the Civil Rights Commission and it seemed as if the limbo would last forever. I needed to do something to get the wheels back in motion. To make it known that I hadn't gone away. I decided to hold a press conference outside of one of the entrances to the mall. In an effort to bring awareness in the city,

I invited political leaders, members of the press, and asked Darold, my lawyer, to address the issues of the case. About half of the people I invited came, and the *Rocky Mountain News* gave me front page coverage on the business section the next day. Channel 7, one of the local TV stations, also interviewed me and I was a lead story the next day on their broadcast. I also made drive-time news on the radio. I had achieved my goal.

I was in my office at the store the next day when the phone rang. "Hello?" I said expectantly, thinking it would be another reporter. They had been calling all morning.

"You're pushing too hard. Go back to Africa or you're a dead woman," a menacing male voice said, and the line went dead. I could barely breathe as a fear unlike any I had ever known seized me. My eyes darted around the room as if he was already there, ominously waiting for me to notice him. I slowly stood and moved towards the doorway that lead out into the store. No one was there except Stasia, one of my sales people. I called to her for help and she ran towards me.

"I just got a death threat," I said and reached for her arm to steady myself.

The police arrived within minutes of our call and I tried to describe the voice as accurately as possible. "It was a male voice." I said, shuddering at the memory of his voice in my ear. "He sounded rough, sort of uneducated, I think." I couldn't picture a voice like that coming from someone in a tie sitting in an office. It was the voice of someone from the dark side who wore a constant sneer. I knew I had never heard the voice before and never wanted to hear it again. My fear was almost primal and I was suddenly afraid for my son, Mengasha, too. What had I gotten us into? Would I ever get us out of it?

The police took the threat very seriously and called regularly to check on me. I was very grateful for their concern.

The next few months went by in a blur of worry and anxiety. I thought I would explode at any moment from the pressure and constant stream of thoughts that pounded my brain. To compound it all, I walked to and from my store hyper-aware of any strange person that might be lingering nearby. I couldn't feel the sun on my face for the shadows that followed me. I started to feel afraid of leaving home and just stopped going anywhere, except to the store. The fear of losing all that I had earned materially was now running a close second to losing my life or that of my son. I tried so hard to not let it rule me, but it was impossible to shake. I had no control over any part of my existence any longer.

As the trial date approached, I started to feel almost relieved. I just wanted it to be over, regardless of the outcome. I wanted my life back in some shape or form. The possibility of having closure after all this time was ever-present in my mind. I had almost forgotten about the Civil Rights Commission filing—and then the letter came. I read it twice because my brain couldn't register the words. The Commission had dismissed my case. With all of the media coverage and attention my court case had been getting, I had never imagined that the Commission would dismiss the case. I still had fears that it could be dismissed any day by the judge, but the eviction was so obviously a violation of my civil rights that I had every expectation that the Commission would agree. It hit me with a force I hadn't expected. The tears came back and this time I was sure that they would not stop no matter what I did.

The waiting and postponements would go on until December of 1998. It wasn't until then that the judge officially said that the case would not be dismissed and set the trial for January, 1999. From the time I received the eviction notice from the Tabor Center until the case was finally put before a jury was nearly three years. I spent the six-month postponement periods expectantly waiting for my day in court, only to have the judge postpone the trial again. It was complete and total hell. Over the course of this time, I went from a vivacious, outgoing person to a withdrawn recluse. I had a cloud that hung over me during every waking hour. It even followed me into my dreams on the nights that I could sleep. Sometimes it took the form of a vast hole that I could inadvertently step into at any moment—one that could swallow me whole. It finally did take the form of anxiety attacks that rendered my body useless and landed me in the hospital more than once. My body physically could not function at such a high rate of constant stress. I was warned repeatedly by doctors that something had to give. But what could it be? Africa House was my life and my lifelong dream and I couldn't walk away or escape it without giving it up. That wasn't a choice for me. Especially when I was finally so close.

During this time, the other merchants in the mall who had always been a source of support had turned away. They didn't want to be involved, and I couldn't really blame them. Most of my friends grew tired of the melodrama and stopped calling. My life ground to a screeching halt with a brief phone call from yet another lawyer. He called to say the trial had been postponed—again. I couldn't make any plans for the future when my future was a moving target. I just wanted to die. I was even placed on suicide watch at one point.

Looking back at those dark, sad days, I really can't recall where the strength to go on came from. The only thing I could cling to was my son and the fierceness of my belief in standing up against a wrong. Not letting them beat me and steal my dream. I knew it was a cause worth fighting for and that my dad would have done the same thing. I had rights and those rights were being violated. My reputation as a human being was on the line and I had to continue to fight.

Chapter 7

In this corner . . .

I'll have to, as you say, take a stand—something towards shaking up that system. . . . Despair . . . is too easy an out.

—Paule Marshall

"United States District Court for the District of Colorado, 96-S-2516, *The Guides, Limited, doing business as Africa House and Foote v. Yarmouth Group Property Management, Inc. and Tabor Center Associates.*[1] Appearances, please."

"Good morning, your Honor. Darold Killmer and David Miller of Miller, Lane, Killmer and Greisen on behalf of Ms. Foote who is present in court."

"Good morning, your Honor. Dov Grunschlag."

"James Aab."

[1] Chapters 7-10 are taken from legal court documents. These are direct lifts from the trial transcripts.

"Representing the defendants, Dan Hill, Art Fong on behalf of Tabor Center Associates and Yarmouth Property Management Group."

"This matter is called for trial this morning. We also have present the jury panel."

"We have a panel of 28 jurors, your Honor."

"Twenty-eight jurors. All have been qualified, duly qualified, by the clerk?"

"Yes, they have."

"The case is called for trial this morning."

And so it began, at long last. I was in court and seated at the table beside my lawyers, Darold Killmer and David Miller. My stomach was tied in a knot that spoke of both my nervousness and excitement. There had been so many times over the last three years that I had thought I would never see this day. I had imagined it over and over—and then the image of my sitting where I was on that day became overshadowed by my assumption that the case would be dismissed. I had fought until it seemed that no fight was left in me. Now I was finally in the ring—fighting for the title—the right to stay in business. The right to be treated equally as a human being. The right to preserve a dream that had been mine for over 30 years. We were finally in our respective corners ready for the match up.

Jury selection took all morning and I closely watched each person's face as they answered the many questions put forth by the judge and attorneys. A homemaker, a college professor, a retiree, a computer specialist, a geologist, a nurse, a grocery store checker—just people, like me, trying to make an honest living. As the morning wore on, the list gradually narrowed down to 12. They were sworn in, given their orders—including keeping their distance from all of us seated at the counsel tables—and we broke for lunch. The trial officially began in earnest in the afternoon.

"Well, good afternoon. I am Darold Killmer. My partner David Miller is with me today, and together we are proud to represent Tseghe Foote, who is also sitting at counsel table. . . . This case is an interesting and important case. The parties, as mentioned, are Tseghe Foote and Africa House. She is a businesswoman now in the second decade of running a business in the downtown Denver area. A business where she sells retail, African-oriented art and imports. Things that indicate the culture of Africa. Sculptures and things of that nature. The defendants are the Tabor Center, the owners of the major Denver retail shopping center, and a major national property management corporation called Yarmouth Group. So the owners and the property managers are the defendants in the case. And the issues of the case, as mentioned by Judge Sparr on a couple of occasions, are interesting and important as well. Juries are often called upon to decide cases that are important to the parties, a breach of a contract or maybe a tax issue or something like that. And those are important to the parties, but these issues, equal protection of the laws and the equal opportunity for success in running a business, and the most fundamental of our civil rights are important obviously to the parties, but they are important to our community as well, and I think that, frankly, as jurors and as a jury, you are fortunate to be able to serve this important role. It's a major commitment on your behalf, but it's a major responsibility too, and we appreciate your undertaking it."

As Darold presented his opening argument, my eyes were again riveted to the 12 people who now held my fate in their hands. As my name was mentioned, one or two of them would glance over at me, smile slightly, and then quickly turn their attention back to Darold. I watched their eyes take in the Tabor Center representatives too, as their misdeeds were presented. I could sense their efforts at impartiality. The tension was thick and lay across my shoulders like a wet blanket. I wanted to appear professional and not wear my desperation on my sleeve. I also tried to avoid looking at Dan Hill and the other guy from the Yarmouth Group's corporate office. There was too much emotion there. If I was going to keep it together, it was best to not relive that anger. "Just don't go there," I kept telling myself.

". . . (s)o ultimately, of course, we are going to ask you to return a verdict in favor of Africa House in this case, and why is this case any different than a normal landlord/tenant dispute? . . . It's important really at three levels. . . . One, of course, it's important to her business. Had she been evicted, and even the fact that she was moved . . . has caused economic consequences to her business, serious economic consequences. There will be expert testimony about just how much those economic consequences are, and that's an important element of damage. But another element of damage which I suggest is more important is the effect it's had on Ms. Foote personally . . . and that's . . . more important than the actual lost sales. In fact, she was . . . mistreated, and the evidence will show that, but to her credit she has been able to land on her feet running. The lost sales would have been more had she actually done nothing and allowed herself to be kicked out, and the effect . . . on her I think [is] even bigger than the lost sales.

"But it's also an important case for your community, and that's the third element. . . . You, as the conscience of the community, will be asked to evaluate what is the proper remedy. You are the judge of the facts, and you are given an opportunity to provide some remedy, if you find that a wrong needs to be righted. And we . . . [suggest] in closing argument that there has been a wrong here, and that you right it. And unfortunately the legal system allows a jury only to award money. The jury can't award leases or anything like that. It's just money. And if you find that our evidence supports that theory of the case, that in fact there was race discrimination, which was one of the reasons they had decided to kick her out, then in fact that's illegal and a remedy is appropriate. . . . If they don't prove their affirmative defenses . . . then you are obligated to award Africa House and Tseghe Foote damages. . . . And we will ask you to speak to those issues and to speak clearly and firmly and tell the defendants and others in this community that they can't do this. They can't do this in this country. Thank you."

I sucked in my breath. His statement had been powerful and the jurors seemed to be momentarily frozen in their spots as his speech ended. The brief reverie was ended abruptly as Judge Sparr brought us back with his booming voice, "Defendants wish to make an opening statement at this time?"

As the Tabor Center counsel rose and began his speech, I could feel my face grow flushed with anger. "Keep your cool, Tseghe," my little internal voice told me, but it was almost impossible. I was infuriated by the injustices these people had heaped upon me. It was so personal, as if they had specifically pointed at me and said, "We don't like you or your store because you are not us. You are black and African." Their "Defendants Brief in Support of Motion for Summary Judgment" had prominently proclaimed, before anything else, that I was a black, single, African immigrant woman. I was clearly discardable to them. And now they were going to try to cover that up to save themselves.

"Members of the jury, my name is Dov Grunschlag, and I represent the Tabor Center Associates and the Yarmouth Group. . . . Let me start by going to the bottom line of what I believe the evidence will show. I believe it will show conclusively that Dan Hill, Dee Torres, Karl Ehrlich, the individuals you have heard mentioned here as the people who did discriminatory things, that these people did not discriminate against Africa House based on race or any other factor that should not be taken into account in business transactions.

"They had no interest whatsoever in kicking her out of the Tabor Center. No reason will be suggested to you in the evidence as to why this shopping center in which she operated for a number of years would not want her to continue to operate there. There would be no business reason for that. No business reason will be shown. There were vacancies, the center looks to fill those vacancies, and they were trying to continue to do so. There was a need and an intent to relocate her from the space that she was occupying once the General Nutrition Centers agreed to come into the space, which the evidence will show they picked out, because they liked it for their purposes, and were willing to sign up for a lease of ten years under which, for the first five years, they would pay more than double the rent that Africa House was paying as a temporary tenant."

I guess the eviction notice had only been my imagination! I gritted my teeth and followed Dov Grunschlag's well-tailored back as he paced in front of the jurors. Why hadn't they just told me that they had a tenant for my space who could pay more? I might have been upset over it, but it certainly wouldn't have lead to this. And they had never once offered another space to me. They had just sent that guy in to measure and told me I was out when I confronted them. It hit me how difficult this trial was going to be to sit through. It was next to impossible to watch the people who had tried to destroy me lie about it all so convincingly. I wondered if the steam coming out of my ears was visible to the jurors. In a way, I hoped it was.

". . . (y)ou will have to conclude, we believe," he continued, that people like Dan Hill, Dee Torres, Karl Ehrlich, you will see them all. You will look them right in the eye, that these people not having a business reason to kick out Africa House, had a racial animus or basis, and I don't think you will conclude that. Thank you for your attention."

I wondered what he would conclude their reason was. That would be interesting to see. What fairy tale they had concocted for themselves. As he took his seat, Grunschlag glanced over in my direction and I could have sworn he nodded at me. It was like he was saying, "There! What do you have to say about that? Put that in your pipe and smoke it!" My face felt flushed again with anger. This was going to be the longest week of my life.

The judge called a recess and the jury left the room. The lawyers and the judge went through some motions on different exhibits. I just wanted to be free. To run from the room screaming. After all of the months of waiting and waiting for this judge to hear my case, wondering if it would be dismissed, I had had enough. I could tell by his rulings and facial expressions that he didn't really believe in my case. I wanted to shake him. Grab his robe and say, "What part of this isn't clear to you?" But, I sat quietly with my hands in my lap while my fantasies of acted-upon aggression dance in my head.

The first witness for my side was called after recess. We had decided to bring in one of my customers, a Harvard-educated, well-respected Colorado Court of Appeals judge and art collector, to testify about the quality of my art. Judge Raymond Dean Jones.

David Miller: ". . . I want to ask how you compare Ms. Foote's shop, the Africa House at the Tabor Center, with the other shops you mentioned across the country?"

Judge Jones: "I can honestly say none of the shops, and they are very good, and most of them are in very good upscale commercial districts, none of them can compare to her presentation and quality. Just cannot. And the quantity of goods. I mean this is not a place that someone set out for the weekend or for last month and maybe they will make it to next month. This is, some of it, gallery quality."

And then came an attorney, Daniel Hoffman. Even though they had been subpoenaed to appear, I appreciated their words so much. I had always been proud of my store, but now I had two well-respected citizens of Denver stating in open court what a unique and upscale store Africa House was. It felt good and their words flowed over me like a sweet song. I felt relaxed again as they spoke. My beautiful store—that's what this was all for. Tabor Center be damned.

Suddenly, it was my turn. The song stopped like someone had removed the needle from the record and I felt the fingers of fear slip slowly around my neck. They weren't gripping me, just silently letting me know they were there. I walked to the stand like a wooden soldier and took the oath. I sat down and ran my tongue across my dry lips. I glanced around for a glass of water and Darold handed one to me. He knew I was scared.

He started out asking me fairly easy questions and I could feel myself calming a bit as I spoke of growing up in Ethiopia, my family, my dream of owning an art gallery that started at 14. He took me through moving to America, going to Denver Technical College for business classes, working at May D&F. A real trip down memory lane. We covered the entire chronology of Africa House. From opening in the Tivoli to moving to Cherry Creek and then the Tabor Center. My life to this point. It was easy so far. I knew this stuff and I knew it was all important to building my case. Making the jury understand who I was and what Africa House meant to me.

We got all the way up to my last buying trip to Africa and my securing a small business loan before the day ended. I was exhausted. My head ached and my feet hurt in the new shoes I was wearing for the first time. I just wanted to have a glass of wine and soak in the tub. It was only Monday and I had at least four more days to go.

I got to court the next day and my nervousness overtook my weariness. I was first on the stand again and we had decided that I would bring some pieces from the store for the jury to see. I was definitely in my element with this. The judge decided that the pieces would be displayed during the first recess and not be admitted into evidence. I climbed into the witness box—I had chosen more comfortable shoes today!—and Darold started his questioning.

"One thing I have noticed is that each piece of work has an Africa House card on it and a description of the piece. For example, this one says a Kuamamua doll, handmade by the Ashanti tribe in Ghana. These were given to expectant mothers to bring good luck to pregnancies and to young girls to render them fertile. Why do you put such tags on the artwork like that?"

"Because I feel it's educational if the public knows what it's for, it helps to sell the products." I answered. "Without information it's not just a piece of art, but they need to know, you know, where it comes from, how it's done and just educational—for educational purpose." I was getting pretty good at this.

Soon, however, the questioning took an inevitable turn. I began to recount the events leading up to my eviction as Darold posed questions.

As soon as I started to speak about how the Tabor Center management had ignored me for months and relayed the story of the strange man in my office at Africa House, I felt something start to fold up inside of me. All of the hurts, lies, and uncertainties that had been dragging on for years by this point began to make their way to the surface. Emotionally, I was wrecked and had been for the last couple of years. Something at my core had shifted irrevocably and I knew that I wasn't the same person I had been. The questions led me to slip backwards and relive the events in the present tense. I had rehashed the story with my lawyers countless times, but it was different to be here, in front of 12 people who would decide the fate of my life and my store. I forced myself to focus on Darold and stay rooted in the courtroom. I couldn't afford to lose it here and now.

At about 10:30a.m., Darold gave me a break to bring Kathy Scheuerman, a friend and former employee to the stand. She was catching a plane to the Super Bowl, where she was hosting an event, that day. I could tell she was nervous and I was so grateful to her for coming. I knew it was hard for her and I had learned that most people just don't want to get involved, but I am sure that her words that day helped my case. She had been there during those first few days—the day the man was in the store, the days I returned from many meetings with Dan. She had seen me through so much.

"Do you know whether or not after these phone calls with her attorney she later went down and met with the Tabor Center people?" David Miller asked her.

"She did, yes."

"And how do you know that?"

"Because I came in to watch the shop for her."

"And when she returned from that meeting, do you know how long it took to get back to the store?"

"Um, it was about a two-hour meeting because I went in about 3:00 and left about 5:00."

"And when she returned, what was her emotional state?"

"She was very upset. Her voice was quivering, her body was slightly shaking."

Her testimony continued and I again felt transported as I listened. I remembered the day she was talking about so vividly. They had just told me that I was out. That I had no options. Listening to her describe my emotional state, it hit me. I am not crazy. This did happen to me and it was wrong. I had someone who had been there and who corroborated my testimony. I looked over at Dov Grunschlag and team and they were all studying the papers in front of them. I wondered if they seriously thought that anything they could ask Kathy would make her perspective, or that of the jury, shift.

"Is it fair to say the events in the Tabor Center in September of 1996 have lasted even to the present time with respect to how they have affected

Ms. Foote?" David Miller asked as his examination drew to a close.

"Yes."

Kathy was cross-examined with no new revelations and she departed for her plane. She waved at me slightly as she hurried for the door. I wanted to jump up and hug her.

Then, I was called back to the stand. I couldn't wait for the day to be over. I got up to the part in my story where I had Pat McHenry and Stuart Schwartz looking for property for me when it came time to recess for lunch. I felt good because I was at least half down with my time on the stand. It was stressful, but I was determined because I had waited for so long to have my time in court. I used the lunch time break to recollect myself and attempt to calm my nerves.

We finished up my testimony fairly quickly after lunch and then it was time for me to be cross examined. I could almost hear the snorts coming out of Dov Grunschlag's nose as he approached. I was the red cloth and he was the bull. I shuddered in fear.

He started in right away trying to establish that my issues were with Dan Hill, not the Tabor Center at large. He suggested that since I had had a good working relationship with Monika Foley even after the Tabor Center was purchased by the Yarmouth Group, that the Tabor Center wasn't the problem. He fired the questions at me so fast that I barely had time to think. I was right in the middle of one of those courtroom dramas on TV, but this time it was real. He took me in circles, dipping me, dropping me to the floor—only to pick me up and drop me again. My tongue was tangled in my mouth. Everything was moving so fast. I answered a question and he would pull out the transcript and show me words I had said months ago. Words I couldn't remember. I started to wonder if I was making sense at all. I looked at Darold and David, my eyes pleading with them, "Make this stop!" They nodded at me, giving me reassurance. I had to stay strong. Too much was at stake now.

Finally, it was over. I was shaking with rage. I could barely revel in being able to step down from the witness stand.

"You did just fine," Darold said and patted my arm when I got back to the table. I smiled at him, but my stomach had soured. The judge called a recess and I went straight outside to the courthouse steps and gulped the fresh air like water when you are thirsty. The sun was shining and the Colorado sky was bright blue in the January cold. Hope. The sky said hope.

Phil Pankoff was next on the stand and he was able to corroborate my testimony that I was being kicked out and given no other options. That boxing bell went off in my head again—Ding! Ding! Maybe this was a round that was ours.

Next up was Dan Hill. My lawyers had decided to call him as an adverse witness. It all went okay for the first bit and then I could see Dan start to squirm. Darold was going in for the kill just like Grunschlag had done to me. Dan tried to avoid the questions or rephrase his answers so that it wouldn't seem like he had said some of the more hurtful things.

"Now the name Africa House negatively portrayed the quality of her merchandise in your opinion, correct?"

"No."

"Well, no—"

"I didn't say negatively portrayed. I said I thought it could be improved."

"Oh."

"I said that it doesn't accurately portray the same quality that her merchandise does."

It was almost painful to watch. He was so obviously uncomfortable and being forced to testify like this in front of his boss. And, I knew how he must be feeling because I had been in his shoes just hours earlier. His answers started to dwindle down to "I don't knows" and "I can't remembers." The deterioration was literally happening before our eyes.

Then, the day drew to a close and I wearily headed home and had a good, long cry.

Chapter 8

"Float Like a Butterfly . . ."[1]

No pain, no palm; no thorns, no throne; no gall, no glory; no cross, no crown.

—William Penn

Dan was up first on the stand again the next day. Darold began with questions about the Tabor Center's marketing plan. The plan's marketing opportunities identified the downtown workers and called for unique attractions versus a typical mall. It called for the Tabor Center to become a strong draw for people looking for an uncommon gift or item. When Darold pressed him on why the GNC would fit this plan better than Africa House, Dan again was uncomfortable. He squirmed in his seat and tried to make the point that he wasn't there when the plan was developed, that he still felt the Tabor Center needed more national merchants. More vitamins than unique gifts.

It got even more interesting as Darold questioned him about the fact that another GNC franchise had existed in the Tabor Center and had failed.

[1] Quote taken from Muhammad Ali.

"And company-wide, you didn't—you didn't even tell Dee Torres there had previously been a GNC, did you?" Darold asked.

"I don't recall. You have to understand when GNC was here previously it was prior to 1990, and I do not know under what situation they left the Tabor Center, but many national tenants, once a department store leaves a shopping area and there is no department store presence, they all leave, so it's kind of irrelevant. It's a totally different set of circumstances."

"You are saying the previous sales history of the exact same company selling the exact same product in the exact same shopping center is completely irrelevant because it had been a few years earlier?"

"Not completely irrelevant, but the market had changed dramatically. This is a totally different environment we are operating in back to when the prior GNC was there."

"To not even making an effort to find the sales figure?"

"It made an effort, but I am not sure that information is that critical given the circumstances."

It was insane. They had used the excuse of my sales not being strong enough to deny me a long-term lease, only to bring in a franchise that had failed in the same location a few years before. Then, they hadn't even bothered to check their financials. I had so obviously been singled out and now the picture was being painted in detail. It was torture sitting there listening to it all. I wanted to scream out at Dan one moment and kiss him the next. It hurt me to hear his words, but his answers were helping to prove my case.

The next line of questioning led to e-mails between Dee Torres, Dan, and a few other people in the Yarmouth Group organization. The exchange was about the termination of my lease—and that was the term they used "termination." Not "relocation." Dan tried to say that he was talking only about my current lease and location, but then ended up admitting that he had wanted a lawyer to look at my lease before they terminated me.

". . . and you say about the second sentence about Africa House in 322, 'This tenant, Africa, is on original term expired 9/30/93. It allows for 15 days relocation slash termination. The language in this lease is highly questionable. There is no question we can relocate her. However, I interpret this language to mean that we have to offer another location before we can terminate.' So you said we can locate her, relocate her, but if we are going to terminate her you read the lease to say we should give her another option first, right?"

"Yes."

"But you are saying it's really—you called it questionable language. You weren't sure, correct?"

"Correct."

"And you said because of that—where do you say—'This is an agreement from two property owners ago, I am going to pass this by our local counsel,' right?"

"Correct."

"So you weren't sure what your options needed to be?"

"Well, more what the process was going to be, because I wasn't familiar with the language in the lease."

"Well, you saw the lease?"

"Yes."

"In fact, you said, 'I read it and it's kind of confusing?'

"Yes."

"But one thing that's not confusing, you can relocate her?"

"Correct."

"So why do you need to run it by your lawyer if there is no question you can relocate her? You are just not sure you can terminate her?"

"I can have every intention of relocating her, but if they don't want to relocate, I am going to come to the point where I am going to have to terminate the merchant and not relocate them because they are not interested in relocating, but I still have the obligation to turn over possession and make every effort to get that space available for the long-term lease that's coming in place."

"Let's apply it to this case. Your story is she had already told Ms. Foote [she had] to be relocated, and that's what she desperately wanted—to stay in the Center?"

"Yes."

"So why are you worried about terminating her when you told her you would keep her and she wanted to stay?"

"My conversation at that stage of the game, I wasn't sure she would stay or not because she was more focused on a long-term lease."

So there it was. The e-mail couldn't lie and neither could Dan since he was under oath. He had used the long-term lease issue as an out, but I had been willing to do anything to stay and he knew it. I looked over at the jury, wondering if it was as clear to them as it was to me. One of them made eye contact with me and quickly looked away. There was no way to tell. I just hoped we could keep up this momentum. I was ready to be vindicated and the main thing I wanted was to hear Dee Torres, Dan Hill, and the others admit they were wrong. That they had wronged me. It shouldn't ever happen to anyone else, ever again.

The next line of questioning was about the termination notice—or eviction I finally received. Darold walked Dan through the process of my receiving four notices and showed proof that this was unusual. He added termination notices for two other businesses into evidence—both of which had only been delivered by certified mail. One copy. Dan said that it may not have been documented that they were hand-delivered too. Touché. But, it was undeniable that my termination notice was the only one served during that period of time in which representatives from Yarmouth Group in San Francisco were sent copies. Dan's answer to that was that he was still learning how things worked; that he was new. The fact that one of the notices was served before and one after mine didn't seem to phase him.

"This is a termination notice to Hi-Tech One Hour Photo and this is a month before you did Ms. Foote's, correct?" Darold asked him, holding the document in front of him as he pointed Dan to the correct place in the evidence book.

"Yes, it is," Dan replied, finding his place and adjusting his position in the chair.

"So this one you cc only the file. You didn't find it important to tell Mr. Ehrlich in San Francisco or even Mr. Dodge or even Ms. Torres?"

"This one was a very strange situation," Dan answered quickly. "We had no intent of having the merchant leave. It was more of trying to clarify exactly who the merchant or the tenant of record was, so I didn't see a need at that time to involve anybody else. We were just trying to establish exactly who the merchant was. If you want me to go into the details I can, but it was a pretty long story." He took a breath as he finished speaking.

"You had no intention of the merchant leaving in that One Hour Photo case, right?"

"Correct. Leaving the premises that they were even in."

I knew he realized what he had just said by the look on his face as he spoke and attempted to correct himself. I could hear that bell again—Ding! Ding! I tried not to smile.

Darold proceeded to lead him through example after example of other tenants who had been given unbelievable deals to stay. There was documentation in each case and Dan plodded along with him. He tried to explain that each instance was different, each case unique, each had a separate reason. All were tenants they really wanted and needed to keep. Tenants they were willing to keep at almost no rent—10 percent of their sales with no side charges. I was having to pay a fixed rent—that no one else was paying—plus 15 percent of my sales if they exceeded $168,000. The very same tenants whose sales were not nearly as strong as mine had been—making less in sales than I did in a space one-third the size of theirs. Even though I had heard this when it was brought out in the discovery phase of the trial, it still stung. I felt my eyes tear up again as Darold brought each exhibit in as evidence and retraced it all for the jury. It was strong evidence and its strength took my breath away. I had been completely and thoroughly betrayed.

We took a recess and it was time for Dov Grunschlag to cross examine Dan. They ran through the litany of questions posed by Darold, attempting to dismiss each one with a line of reasoning they assumed to be sufficient. That my rent-to-sales ratio, by their calculations, was actually too high for them to offer me a long term lease. That I could have taken the short-term lease and ended up with a month-to-month consent. That I was emotional during it all and Dan wanted to work through a broker because of that. All of these reasons why I was crazy and they were just professionals trying to do their job. I knew better and I hoped that the jury would too.

Right before the lunch recess, Dov Grunschlag had Dan Hill look directly at the jury and say that race had no bearing on the decisions made in this case. After all of the liberties he had taken with the truth during his testimony so far, this statement sent chills down my spine. The break was a welcome one.

When we returned, Dan was up again—this time for a redirect from Darold. I watched as his mouth tangled around his words.

". . . one of the points you made on your examination was this so-called holdover language, and tenants can hold over at the end of that lease so long as they don't get kicked out. Do you recall that testimony?"

"Yes."

"But you had already told Ms. Foote that the best you could do on that space was four months because Dee Torres told you you couldn't go for it, right?"

"That was the term of the lease was four months, but that just means typically on a short-term lease that the tenant is making that commitment, it's still a month-to-month lease from the landlord's perspective."

"But on that lease you said that sorry, that was already spoken for, but I can get you through Christmas?"

"It wasn't that certain she was currently negotiating on it. I didn't say she wouldn't have it after that four-month period. If they didn't there was no reason why she couldn't stay."

"You understood she was an established business not a fly-by-night operation?"

"Yes."

"Up [to] and including that October 18th proposal, you had never offered her more than anything but that four-month commitment, correct?"

"In that location?"

"Well, in any location."

"I tried to get her to look at some other locations but she wasn't interested."

"But you never gave her a specific idea, proposal, writing or otherwise, here is a place you can set up your business and run your business for anything more than that four months?"

"No, because she wasn't interested in looking at anything else other than that location."

"And you yourself are the one who said you could never trust a landlord who tells you you can stay beyond the term of the lease. That's like the right of refusal testimony you gave yesterday?"

"Things can change overnight in terms of particular deals coming up."

"It's month-to-month, so that's all you can count on, right?"

"If I was a tenant, that would be the position I would take."

"And that would be the position you would take if you were Tseghe Foote, if you were trying to run your business at the Tabor Center too?"

"On a month-to-month lease, yes."

I heard his words, knew he was attempting to tell the truth, but I knew that he knew better. No business owner would take out a loan secured by their house if they felt their business was only temporary. My intentions had always been to establish myself in a permanent situation. I had been trying to get a long-term lease from them for months prior to their leasing my space out from under me. I had come to the Tabor Center with a promise of a long-term location and had made the fatal mistake of trusting them. Dan Hill knew exactly why I wasn't comfortable with a four-month lease. I wanted to stay and wanted a guarantee in writing that I could. With the loan hanging over me, it would have been suicidal to agree to a temporary arrangement.

Darold next called Karl Erlich. He was the senior vice president of Yarmouth Group and the one Dan had said originally pointed to Africa House (or the sign) and said, "This has to go." As he took the stand, his irritation was palpable. He was an intense, humorless man, and it was obvious that he resented this whole situation. Being called as a witness for my side was just the icing on the cake for him. He eyed Darold suspiciously as he took the stand.

The questioning started and Darold made it clear that Erlich was an adverse witness—as if we all couldn't tell simply by looking at him. His jaw was set and his body rigid. He nearly spat his answers as Darold posed them. Defiance was written all over his face. He wanted to beat us and was furious that he had been called by our side. Darold started the dance by asking some pointed, direct questions that Erlich ducked. It wasn't that he lied so much as simply skirted the truth. The "I can't recall" response was placed on endless loop playback. It was usually followed by a "It could have happened that way." He wouldn't admit anything and barely flinched when Darold pointed to his deposition where he had clearly stated a precise memory of the very same event in question. He would coolly reply, "I cannot testify under oath that it did not happen that way." His eyes followed Darold and shot poisoned darts through the space between them. It was truly unbelievable to watch. A tension filled the room like none I had felt so far. It found its way inside of me and beat inside my chest like a drum. Darold was taking his predatory role in stride. I was so glad to have him on my side. The hatred in Erlich's eyes made me shudder each time he looked my way. I wrapped my arms around myself to ward off the chill.

Darold worked quickly to establish that their wanting me out of the Tabor Center had little to do with national presence, or even sales figures for that matter.

"You recall that Brooks Brothers, their sales per square foot was less than Africa House?" Darold asked.

"On sales per square foot, that's correct."

"And Brooks Brothers was a national tenant. Was. They are gone now?"

"Right." Erlich's face was like stone. He obviously did not like being forced into a corner.

By the end of his testimony and cross-examination by Grunschlag, his face was red with rage, and before Darold could stand for his redirect, Erlich exploded.

"I am going to ask you whether you can look the jury in the eye and tell them whether race had anything to do with anything you did in this matter?" Grunschlag asked, in what had become his customary manner.

"Race did not have anything to do with my decision making in this matter in any way, shape or form. And, frankly, it's disgusting that we are having to be here and do this. I come from an interracial marriage, and this really bothers me. That somebody could try to pull a fast one like this. This is wrong." He looked directly at me as he ended his speech. He was nearly shaking in the fit of anger that had overtaken him. The strength of his emotion reached across the room to my place at the plaintiff's table. I was gripped with fear and shocked by his vehemence. I felt bile rise to the back of my throat and I took quick breaths to hold it down. Then, I realized what was happening. He felt like a hypocrite and was incredibly angry at being put in that position. How must it feel to be a man married to a woman of a different race, yet be accused of racial discrimination? He must have felt he was above the accusation based on his choice of a spouse. What he was forgetting is that you have to live all of your life without bias—and not just your personal life.

The day was dragging on and I sat in my seat impassively as a man I had had discussions with about marketing my business was called to the stand. His testimony was fairly uneventful and Darold had really just called him to testify about the sales potential of Africa House. Soon it was time for a recess and I was bone-tired. These were fast becoming the longest days of my life.

When we returned to the courtroom that afternoon, Dee Torres was called to the stand. I was dreading her testimony. I knew it would cut me to the quick and I tried to pull from my energy reserves in preparation. She was also being called as a hostile witness by my attorneys. It was an interesting strategy, but one that I knew Darold was confident would work. So far the ones he had called had helped my case. Now it was Dee's turn. I shuddered involuntarily as she took the stand. My mind flashed back to her voice on the phone as she spoke her name into the microphone. The venom of her words as she told me, "I don't deal with people who sell less than $800,000 a year" came racing back to me. She had been so mean and ruthless through this whole thing, and now I had to face her—live. I was seeing her in person for the very first time, and I was actually surprised to see how attractive she was. The only thing that betrayed her good looks was an underlying hardness to her face. She had a "don't mess with me" look about her, and her pantsuit spoke volumes about her no-nonsense approach. She was obviously a very tough woman who cared very little about the people she hurt to achieve success. I shuddered again. What a group they were! I pictured the jury looking at Karl Erlich with his hatred and Dee Torres with her venom and holding them up against me. I weighed about 95 pounds and knew that any anger I felt wasn't visibly apparent. I was mostly just hurt and tired of the whole thing. They were out for blood. It was like David and Goliath. These two powerful angry people against little old me. Maybe I *was* crazy.

The exchange between Dee and Darold became heated almost immediately, causing the judge to intervene.

". . . so it's a fair statement that Yarmouth Group initiated the contact with GNC that came to be the lease at Tabor?"

"Yes, that's my job."

"That's okay. Nothing wrong with that. Just trying to get how this came up. At that point, in fact, when they said they were interested, they started to give you some limitations including the size of the space?"

"I don't know exactly how it came about. I know what size GNCs are. There are 4,800 of them across the country."

"You knew then they would be looking for about 1,000, 1,500 square feet?"

"Yes."

"You knew there were several spaces including 322 at the Tabor Center?"

"I don't know if there were several. There were a couple, yes."

"Well, there is more than two, right?"

"I don't know the exact number."

"I am not asking for the exact number."

"There were other spaces."

"Okay. And one of them was Africa House?"

"Was space 322, yes."

"But space 320, for example, which at various times has been inhabited by Candy Barrel or Software, Etc., that's also within—"

"That space was occupied in July of 1996. I wouldn't have shown that that had a permanent lease in it."

"I understand, Ms. Torres, but I am just asking about the property you are responsible for and what types of spaces may have fit that specification. Okay. I am not arguing with you. It's the same size, right, it's within the specification?"

The Court: "Why don't you just list all the spaces in Tabor Center that are the same size and that will answer the question."

"There are 50 spaces."

The Court: “Is that what you want?”

“That would be good,” replied Darold.

The Court: “Okay. If you remember them. If you don’t—generally. There are a whole bunch of spaces in Tabor Center that fit the specifications for this?”

“Yes,” Dee finally replied. “And there are spaces that can be configured differently as well. You do that for, you know, so there is always opportunity, so I guess I can’t list all the spaces.”

The Court: “That answers the question.”

“I think so. Thank you, your Honor.”

Dee was defensive for the remainder of her testimony and Darold had to push and prod to get her to answer questions directly. When he brought up the subject of her e-mail to Karl Erlich, she bristled. The e-mail exchange, as Dan Hill had testified, was initiated by Dee and was very damaging. Her choice of words came back to haunt her as we sat there in the courtroom that day. I watched raptly as Darold asked her to refer to Plaintiff’s Exhibit 5.

“This is a series of three e-mails exchanged between you and Mr. Hill all on September 9th, 1996. You recognize them as such?”

“Um-hm.”

“. . . the first one says ‘Hi, Dan and John,’ and you are asking him ‘Dan, do I generate the termination paperwork for Africa House, or do you walk a letter up to the space that informs them they will be leaving.’ Is that what you asked him?”

“Yes, that’s what’s written.”

"Then you put in parenthesis, 'Could it be that easy?'

"Um-hm."

"In fact, you found out that was that easy. That's exactly what happened?"

"What I meant is many times when you terminate a tenant it could be a partnership, the partnerships could be in different states. It could be a situation of where—I have had it happen—a divorce where you have to find a spouse who doesn't know where the other spouse is. Terminations of people and the lease or the legal term of termination can be very difficult if you don't know where the people are, so it's by what I wrote was could it be that easy is could it be that convenient, that that one person who is on the lease is also in the Center. We have partnerships where the partners work in different states. So walking a letter to the space in the same mall would make it easy."

I knew she had walked by my store and seen me there many times, even though we had never met. She knew—oh, too well—that I, as the owner, was always there. My signature was right there on the lease. No partnership. Just me as a solitary owner. What was she talking about—partnerships or me not being in the Center? It was so obvious to me that she was covering her tracks and was being caught in that lie.

"And, in fact, you found out that was that easy with Africa House, right?" Darold continued.

"She was in the space, yes."

"And Mr. Hill responds to you on the second e-mail he would handle it, you don't have to, and his response to him is the first e-mail at that page, which is at the top—do you see that?"

"Yes."

"You are telling him GNC is pretty hot to trot, wants to be open for the holidays?"

"Yes."

"Time seems to be of the essence to you; is that a fair statement?"

"Yes."

"In your second paragraph it's—you talk about how long it's going to take or how quickly you can kick out Africa House, and you do say the deal with GNC does provide we must give Africa House 30-days' notice, although I had Phil take a look at the kickout and he read it was 15 days not 30. I just gave us some extra cushion."

"What you are talking about is the lease kickout for Africa House?"

"Right. Which she had agreed to, right."

"And you are saying this is good news, I just saved 15 days on this?"

"Yes."

She was caught. It was right there in written word, signed by her that they were kicking me out—not just relocating me as Dan Hill had tried to say. This was the one overt piece of evidence we had showing that fact. Nothing about this whole situation was completely obvious to an outsider, but the wording of that e-mail was unmistakable. I was being terminated, not just moved to accommodate a national chain, like they wanted me and the jury to believe. And they couldn't explain why. Yes, she went through a whole process with Darold and Dov Grunschlag during her questioning, trying to say it was my sales. That I wasn't selling enough to warrant a long-term lease. Even though that wasn't exactly the truth either, did it warrant them kicking me out after five years of being a good tenant who paid rent on time—even over paid at times? I was doing better than Brooks Brothers for God's sake! What did they want? The e-mail told it all. They wanted me out and that was it.

During her questioning by Grunschlag he posed the question of race to her. The same one he had asked Erlich. Her response flattened me to my chair in shock—she was married to a minority, too, and had two small children who were minorities. It truly seemed that she had no idea what she had done. This was the kind of discrimination that made my hair stand on end. The kind that was almost silent—so silent that even the perpetrators barely realized what they were doing. It was discrimination of the most dangerous breed.

Dee left the stand and Jana Thorpe was called. She was the owner of the Mountain Man Fruit and Nut franchise located next door to me on the second floor once I had to move. She testified that she was offered a long-term lease even though her rent-to-sales ratio would have been 16 percent. Mine was 15 percent and I was considered too much of a risk, according to Dee Torres. That discrepancy in my treatment alone proved that the Tabor Center had committed a wrong against me, but then she had something else to say.

"What kinds of conversations about long-term leasing did you have with Ms. Torres . . . ?"

"A wide variety. My main concern was what tenants would be my neighbors, and what long-term tenants would be signed. I didn't want to sign a long-term lease until I knew who else would be signing long-term leases or had a good knowledge of what types and varieties of stores would be in the Center and where they would be located."

"So in these conversations did you discuss with Ms. Torres whether or not Ms. Foote would be offered a long-term lease?"

"Yes. We did have conversations."

"During those conversations what did Ms. Torres say?"

"She said that Africa House would not be offered a long-term lease."

"Did she say why Africa House would not be offered a long-term lease?"

"It didn't fit the proposed image of the Tabor Center."

". . . What did you understand her testimony to be when she said Africa House wouldn't fit the image of Tabor Center?"

Mr. Grunschlag: "Objection. What her conclusion was was irrelevant."

The Court: "Overruled."

"The first thing that I thought when the word image—Africa House—didn't fit the image of the Tabor Center was that Africa House was a store owned by a black person that sold things from Africa and had black customers. That's the first thing that I thought."

"Did you have an occasion to speak with Ms. Foote after Africa House was served its termination, and did you have an ability to observe her emotional demeanor?"

"Yes."

"Can you describe for the jury Ms. Foote's emotional demeanor after having been served with a notice of termination?"

"She was very upset, very confused, very upset."

I wanted to cheer. This was it. Jana Thorpe was enough to fill my heart with hope. I hadn't imagined this whole thing after all. Here was a businesswoman, like myself, who had seen the events happen firsthand and could support it all. No matter what Dee Torres, Karl Erlich, or Dan Hill said, what they had done to me was an overtly bad thing. I beamed at her as she left the witness stand.

Pat McHenry, the leasing agent, was up next and the judge decided to call it a day and save her testimony until the next morning. He adjourned court and I stretched a bit to alleviate the stiffness in my back and neck. I had been holding my body so tightly all day as I sat in that chair with negative energy flowing around me like a current. Now, the day was over and I was ready to get out of that room. I turned and spied Norma sitting in the viewing area, talking to someone I didn't recognize. I caught her eye and she smiled back at me and motioned for me to come over her way. "Do you feel like grabbing dinner somewhere?" I asked, once she had bid good bye to her new courtroom buddy. "I am feeling too wound up to go home and could use a glass of wine."

"Sure!"

We headed out of the courtroom and I immediately felt lighter. Three days had passed and I already dreaded coming back the next day. It made me realize how vehemently I wanted this whole ordeal to be over.

I was back in my seat in the courtroom before I felt I had even had time to close my eyes. My head felt a little achy from the bottle of wine I had shared with Norma at dinner. I didn't drink very often, so one glass could do me in effectively. I had had more in the neighborhood of two as Norma and I rehashed the day's events over grilled halibut and steamed vegetables.

The first witness called on Thursday was Dr. William Kaempfer. He had a Ph.D. in Economics from Duke University and we had paid him to serve as an expert witness. David Miller handled his questioning and covered the basics of my losses over the years since I had been relocated. He had done some calculations and projections of what I could have made if I had stayed in the same location. It was fairly technical testimony and he actually made a mistake during the examination that caused him to re-calculate his figures on the stand. The defense objected and we had to take a recess to sort out his new testimony. We reached an agreement with the defense that he couldn't increase his projected loss figures, he could only amend his error.

Aab cross-examined him and made an attempt to trip him up in the minutiae of the figures. Kaempfer floundered a bit, but pretty much regained his composure by the end and held firm. It was a bit of a blow to have your expert witness make an open mistake, but I didn't think it would matter all that much in the big picture. I wasn't really concerned with the money anyway. I just wanted them to admit their wrongs and publicly apologize.

Lew Gaiter who had helped me with securing my business loan was called next. He had put together my proposal to the Money Store and the lawyers asked him various questions about whether my having a different space in the Tabor Center would have affected the loan approval and whether or not my having a long-term lease would have mattered. He got a little angry when Grunschlag attempted to insinuate that I had broken some law by not using my loan for precisely what I stated in the application. He straightened Grunschlag out quickly with the explanation that the loan was for operating expenses and any future plans were simply that—plans. He made the point that I would have been very lucky, under the circumstances, to accomplish everything I wanted to do with my business. There was only a short time between my receiving the money and being kicked out. And, once I was evicted, I had to pay the loan right away.

It was good. I hadn't seen or spoken to this man in years, yet he had shown up and rallied to my defense. There was some kindness left in the world. He patted my shoulder as he walked by on his way out. I smiled at him and mouthed "Thanks."

David Fine, the lawyer who had gotten me on the right track at the beginning of this whole thing and had saved my business by filing a court order to stop my removal, was next in the lineup. The purpose of having him testify was to establish that I was indeed being evicted from the Tabor Center and would not have been offered a place on the second floor if it hadn't been for the injunction he filed on my behalf. He could barely get his answers out between objections by Grunschlag for irrelevance or information that was protected under the current lawsuit. Judge Sparr overruled every time and David handled it very well. It was stressful to watch, though, and I also thanked David as he passed by our table at the end. He was a good man and had done well by me.

As David's testimony ended, Darold announced that the plaintiff rested. I exhaled aloud in relief. It would be over soon, very soon. I could hardly believe it. That we were so close to having this whole nightmare reach an end, even if it wasn't in my favor. My gut was telling me that our chances were good and I was bolstered by Judge Sparr's response to Grunschlag's move for judgement.

"We would move for judgment under Rule 50, your Honor." Grunschlag announced.

"Do you have any argument you want to make at this time?" Judge Sparr asked.

"Very briefly."

"All right. In anticipation of the plaintiff's resting, I will allow the motion at this time, unless there is objection," Judge Sparr asked, looking at Darold.

"No objection," Darold replied.

"Go ahead. Make it brief."

"The case has not been made that the plaintiff was refused a long-term lease on any kind of a definitive basis, that she was qualified for a long-term lease, which is a requirement she has to meet, given the standards for giving leases, which has not been disputed. There is no evidence of disparate treatment of the plaintiff, there is no evidence of eviction in the sense of kicking her out, and for the wanting to have her in the Center under any terms and conditions whatsoever. The evidence is to the contrary; that there is relocation that occurred and offered."

"That's a question of fact, isn't it?" the Judge responded.

"Well, I think we—"

"Take the last five minutes of the testimony, and I think you have a question of fact on that issue." Sparr countered.

"Well, this witness is not competent on that issue."

"Nonetheless, that's his testimony. That there was no issue of relocation."

"Well, there was a proposal." Grunschlag was starting to get slightly ruffled by the Judge's challenges. This judge had been nearly backing his every move to this point and he wasn't fully expecting to have to defend himself so strongly.

"And there was an eviction." Sparr added. "There has been other testimony from her. There is clearly a question of fact as to whether or not she was being evicted or relocated."

"There was a proposal. It was undisputed she received the proposal for short-term lease on space 202. And that that could be done and accepted and negotiated and effectuated before the need to evacuate the space at all. And, in any event, that there was no disparate treatment of her relative to anybody else with respect to the need for the space when another tenant was interested in it, or when the landlord wished to lease it to a tenant on a month-to-month lease. There is no evidence that race entered into it. And I think from which that can be inferred, no disparate treatment, no comparative situations of that kind. No other situations where someone not of this race in the similar situation was permitted to remain in the space they occupied when the landlord wished to lease it to someone else. Especially at more than double the rent. That's in brief our motion, your Honor."

"Anything else?"

"Unless the Court would like to hear argument, I am prepared—I could talk for a while, but I just think there is plenty of evidence and there is fact questions; differential treatment at several different levels, not only the failure to give any sort of long-term security, but the attempt to evict her. The evidence is conflicting on this. The testimony is two sides of a coin. You can't believe both sides, and the jury needs to sort that out."

"If nothing else, the Mountain Man Nut and Fruit lady certainly gave evidence, taken in the light most favorable to the plaintiff, with regard to the issue of race, not even considering the circumstantial evidence along those lines," the judge added.

My heart soared. It was the first official hope I had received; the first true justification of all of the pain and stress I had been through over these last couple of years. Now, a conservative judge who had doubted the merit of the case to begin with could see it. I wanted to jump up and scream "YES!" at them all—shake my fist in the air at Erlich and the rest. A smile tugged at my mouth and I couldn't hold it back. What the hell. I had been crying for so many months. I deserved to smile.

They finished their motions and the judge denied the motion to render judgment based on lack of evidence. The trial would proceed and the defense would present their case after lunch.

"This is a very good sign, Tseghe," Darold said to me as we walked out of the courthouse.

"Do you really think so? I am still afraid to get my hopes up."

"I think it is pretty safe to get excited. I don't know what the jury will do, but I don't think we are going to lose this one." He smiled at me and we both started to laugh.

The first defense witness called was Monika Foley. She didn't really add all that much and mostly said she couldn't remember dates,and other information. She bit her lip a lot as she spoke and seemed to be really nervous. I hated that she was being put in this position, but I wasn't mad at her for testifying for the defense. She hadn't really had a choice after all. I just felt a tinge of regret over the fact that our relationship would be altered forever by all of this. She had already stopped shopping at my store. It was one of the expected by-products of being involved in a controversy. I had considered her a friend at one time, but she had moved on to work at Park Meadows and then all of this had come up. The whole thing was just so damned regrettable. I wished none of it had ever happened.

The second defense witness was Pat McHenry, one of the brokers I called for help when I was being evicted. She had also been employed by the former owners of the Tabor Center as the long-term leasing agent there when I first came over from Cherry Creek North.

"I didn't—do not believe that I met Tseghe until after she became a tenant. I do recall going and looking at her store in Cherry Creek prior to us making the decision to allow her to come on in a temporary lease at Tabor Center, but I don't believe I had met her until after she was a tenant."

"But you were the manager at the Shops At Tabor Center, correct?"

"I oversaw the project. I was not the property manager. We have a different structure, for example, than Yarmouth had."

"You are aware that the name of the shop had to be approved by management before?"

"Oh, certainly we knew what the name of the shop was, yes."

"And Trammell Crowe (previous owner of Tabor Center) had absolutely no problem whatsoever with Africa House, correct?"

"We did not have a problem with that name."

"Didn't think that name devalued the property values, correct?"

"Correct."

"Didn't have a problem with her sign, did you?"

"No."

"Wouldn't have allowed her to put the sign up if you didn't think it was appropriate for a tenant?"

"That's correct."

"Is there a review process through which the Tabor Center at that time actually made sure that signs and names were in compliance with shopping center requirements?"

"Yes. We have procedures in place."

"And they are formal procedures, not as though they apply to some people and not others, correct?"

"Yes."

"And, in fact, designers are used?"

"Your Honor, I thought some leeway was appropriate, but this takes the witness off in another direction," Grunschlag interjected.

"I am assuming this is going to the issue of the conditions under which she was brought in to the Tabor Center in the first instance, and I will allow it for whatever it's relevant," Judge Sparr replied.

"Is that correct, Ms. McHenry?" David Miller, who was questioning her, asked.

"That's correct."

"In terms of Miss Foote's shop, you had no problem with how she mixed with the rest of the tenants at the shops, correct?"

"The way I would describe that, if you are—I would say as the temporary tenants went, I think she was one of our higher-quality, temporary tenants. There is a difference between temporary tenants, or very often there is a difference between the merchandising presentation and the marketing done on a temporary tenant retailer versus either a national or a stronger permanent tenant."

"Fair to call Ms. Foote's shop while you were there a strong temporary tenant?"

"Yes."

Pat was a strong witness. She came across as confident and without bias. There was no anger or defiance in her voice, even when my lawyer cross-examined her. She was simply a professional who had gotten caught in the crossfire of this debacle.

Her testimony, although she was a witness for the defense, helped my case enormously. She had been able to establish that the urgency with which I had been forced to find another place—in only nine days—was remarkable. She testified that it normally takes three months to a year to negotiate a lease, but that I obviously had not had that luxury. As she left the stand, I could sense that the courtroom had shifted a bit. Based on her observances, Trammell Crowe had loved having me as a tenant while the Yarmouth Group had taken the same Africa House and found a million reasons for me to leave.

The broker for GNC, Mike McCormick, was called and testified without much ceremony. He basically covered that GNC wanted my space and it was the first choice. Then, after an afternoon recess and negotiations with the judge on how we would wrap the trial up, Tim Gonerka was called. He was a lease negotiator who had managed the Tabor Center for the first nine years it was open. He served as their paid, expert witness on whether I qualified for a long-term lease or not. In fact, what he ended up doing was backing my case by testifying that no good reason existed for my eviction, especially in light of the many vacancies at the center at that time. He also backed up the fact that GNC had been a tenant at the Tabor Center before and had failed. It made me chuckle under my breath. Given the stress of this trial, to sit there and watch the defense call a witness who helped my case was rather comical. I didn't want to let myself get too confident, but both Darold and David had agreed that we were ahead with the jury. Grunschlag had not proved their case so far, and had actually helped ours with his witnesses' testimony.

Next came Phillip Atkinson who worked for the Tabor Center when the whole thing came about. He had been in on one of the conference calls in Dan Hill's office when they had been talking about changing the Africa House name. His main or sole purpose was to establish that Dee Torres and Dan Hill had suggested names that had the word Africa in it. Big deal, I thought. It was completely beside the point and I just looked at Darold and shook my head as Grunschlag questioned him. It had already been established that the same people in question had said the name wasn't glamorous enough and they couldn't explain why. Oh yeah, they had said it was the word "house" that was the problem. Whatever. I had heard enough and was tired and ready for it to be over.

And, my wish was close to being granted. After Atkinson left the stand, Grunschlag announced, "The defense rests." I looked over at the jury to gauge their reaction to this announcement, and they just looked tired. I couldn't really see much relief and I figured that they knew the hard part still lay ahead. They were dismissed while some final motions were heard by the judge. Namely, the defense trying to have the case dismissed. They had a million reasons why I had no case, but I felt that my lawyers had done a great job in proving that I did indeed deserve a chance with the jury. The judge agreed with me enough to deny most of their motions. The only one he agreed with was not awarding pain and suffering—because we had filed as Africa House. He said he couldn't see how a store could have pain and suffering. I thought it was pretty clear that Africa House and I were interchangeable, but no dice. He called a five-minute recess and the closing arguments started up. Darold went first.

Chapter 9

"... Sting Like a Bee."[1]

I knew as well as I knew anything that the oppressor must be liberated just as surely as the oppressed. A man who takes away another man's freedom is a prisoner of hatred, he is locked behind the bars of prejudice and narrow-mindedness. I am not truly free if I am taking away someone else's freedom, just as surely as I am not free when my freedom is taken from me. The oppressed and the oppressor alike are robbed of freedom.

—Nelson Mandela

"Well, good afternoon. First time I have got to talk with you directly since—what was it, a month and a half ago, it seems like. Monday morning. I want to start by thanking you, and I think I can speak on behalf of defendants and their counsel in this part of my closing, probably the last part I will speak on their behalf, but I have to say you have been one of the most attentive juries I have seen. It has been a

[1] Quote taken from Muhammad Ali.

long week and a lot of breaks and sometimes it tends to drag on.

"I also want to insert an apology of sorts here. I know from watching trials myself, watching other lawyers work, and certainly a lot of people have told me before, it's frustrating sometimes to watch a trial from the perspective of the juror. You are required—and you know you have an important job to do—you are required to make an important decision at the end, but it's left up to us to bring the evidence in, and I imagine at various times through the week you have all probably wondered why these lawyers keep asking the same question, why does he keep asking that, we get it, and maybe, on the other hand, you are wondering why doesn't he ask this. This is a real obvious question. I would ask this, and maybe you wanted to do that. That happens. You can never tell when it's going to happen, so I need to apologize for that, for trying. We tried to get the evidence before you that we think is pertinent and important for your decision, so with that introduction, maybe we should talk about the case a little bit.

"You may recall that in the opening statement I suggested to you that the jury is playing, in this case particularly, more so than others, a critical role in an important case than others I think. I suggested that this case was going to turn—we will win or we will lose, the defendants will win or lose—based, I believe, on credibility determinations and the findings of fact on a couple of very important factual disputes. And if you believe the defense version of the facts, then you most assuredly will vote for the defense, but I asked you to commit on Monday morning, and I expect you did so, that if you found the facts in favor of Ms. Foote and Africa House then you would return a verdict which emphasized that.

"And I think it's become apparent that one side in this case is not telling the truth. They can't be. There [are] yes/no disputes on the evidence. Somebody is not telling the truth. And Judge Sparr will read you what's called the charge, the jury instruction, but among those instructions is a significant series of jury instructions that talks about the credibility of witnesses and some guidelines on how you will assess the evidence. You sort of sort through this jungle of conflicting contrasting evidence. Those are very important instructions. Among other things, those instructions tell you that if you believe that a witness testified falsely in any way, you can disbelieve that witness on that point, but not just on that point. You can disregard that witness' entire testimony if you think that that witness has not been being straight with you. And in full force apply that to the testimony of Ms. Foote. In full force apply it to the testimony of every witness that we called to support our case. You apply it to every single witness.

"And the last point in overview I think I want to make is one of focus. I think that there has been some diversion of the issues. There is certainly, you may have thought even more than I am suggesting here, that there has been some irrelevant issues talked about this week, but I think there is at least one that I will highlight at the outset, and that's a comparison between who is a better tenant, Africa House or General Nutrition Center. That's not what this case is about. The General Nutrition Center may be a massive national company and they may have more money. General Nutrition Center has more money, but that's not the issue here. In fact, the focus, what I think this case is going to turn on completely by the end is one issue, one issue only: relocation or kickouts.

"The two versions of the world, the two pictures of the puzzle, as Judge Sparr described at the outset, are two different pictures. Defendant's picture is she misunderstood at all times. Ms. Foote, through either inability to understand or refusal to understand, just didn't get it when they said you have to move from 322 down the hall or downstairs somewhere, but don't worry we are going to relocate you, because that's their sworn testimony, and they are sticking to it, and they even told them, look at the jury this time and tell them that sort of thing, and that's their story. I believe that's false. And what you have to determine is whether that's false too.

"Our story, in stark contrast, absolutely 100 percent opposite of that, is there was no plan to relocate her. Rather, they wanted her to leave. Now admittedly when she stood up to them, I think surprisingly to them, she said you can't do this, they had to come up with some ideas to placate her for a while, but you won't find a shred of evidence, not a scintilla of evidence, that they ever provided her any security except to get her past the Christmas season, and then she was out, and that's what they wanted the whole time, and I think the evidence will support that. They were kicking her out of the center; that's what they were doing.

"Let's review the evidence. First point, there is no dispute, Ms. Foote testified to it, there was no contrary testimony, that she was ignored by the Yarmouth Group for the first five or six months that the new management team took over. The evidence has shown that Yarmouth took over in 1995, but they utilized the personnel really of Trammell Crowe, the company that was there before, the personnel was the same even though Yarmouth took over, but when Yarmouth put their management team in, that was Mr. Hill as the general manager, Mr. Ehrlich become involved from San Francisco, there was no dispute they came in in April and didn't even bother that they introduce themselves until September of 1996; that's when she went to their office and said I feel ignored, but that is undisputed.

"Second point, on September 13th, 1996, Ms. Foote confronted Dan Hill, and this was based upon her sense of something being wrong. She had talked to tenants. One of them had said they are cancelling me. She knew of other tenants they were negotiating with, they were soliciting possibly for a long-term lease, and she is thinking about my future, what's going to happen and why aren't they contacting me. So she goes to find out. That's what Ms. Foote does; she has a question, she asks it. That's her character. And Mr. Hill says at that point, according to his testimony, this is disputed, Ms. Foote doesn't agree with this, but he says what a coincidence you came in today, I was just going to come and see you because a national tenant has taken over your spot and we are going to relocate you, so let's look around. That was Mr. Hill's testimony fairly summarized.

"Ms. Foote, on the other hand, says that's different. Why aren't you talking to me, why can't I get a lease, some sense of security, the detailed discussion about long-term leases hadn't begun, and Mr. Hill responded in a variety of ways including the response that your store really doesn't mix well with the other tenants. Now we have heard testimony through the week that this "mix well" or this phrase "tenant mix" may be a term of art in the retail industry. It's used in a lot of different contexts, but the testimony has a ring of truth in it. This isn't Tseghe Foote's jargon that he is using. Who is more likely to use a phrase like that in the first instance, Mr. Hill, who has significant retail background, or Ms. Foote, an immigrant from Ethiopia who doesn't talk that way?

"The fact is this conversation occurred on September 13th. Well, standing alone a suspicious sort might really get up in arms about this, but it's a minimum disturbing because—this is why it's disturbing: What Mr. Hill says happened, we are going to relocate you, didn't happen. What really happened is you don't really fit the mix here, you don't mix well with the other tenants, tell me a little bit about yourself and I will think about it. And, she invited him up to the store, and for the first time he walked up and saw Africa House. And, as I imagine most of you were, Mr. Hill was impressed. It's very, very nice merchandise, it's very high quality, high-caliber works of African art. And he said well, this is pretty nice, maybe we can do something, I will have Ms. Torres call up. That's not been disputed. That's Ms. Foote's testimony, so Ms. Foote, after this conversation, while initially concerned that he said you don't mix well with the other tenants, that same day after the walk-through he seemed satisfied this was a nice store and maybe something could be done.

"And you heard her testify that even though the passage of eleven days then occurred, from September 13th to September 24th, that's not that big a deal to her because she said they are always a little bit slow, but as long as I have got—it seemed to me I convinced him this is a nice store and we can do something, so she is feeling a little bit more secure at that point.

"September 24th. This is the incident, the insurance guy, the guy in her back room that's measuring her office and moving files and sputters around. This is the insurance lie. And this, frankly, is made up of undisputed evidence too. Ms. Foote testified that she walked in and said who are you, what's this, why are you here. And asked—in fact, asked Kathy Scheuerman, the manager who was watching the store when she was there, and she said the maintenance guy, the manager, Mike Baca of Tabor Center, said he is here trying to reduce insurance rates and he is going to do some measurements.

"It turns out that's what they tell people all the time. Dan Hill testified from the stand that's common in the industry. We don't want tenants to have anxiety before they have to have anxiety. If we are going to rent the space to someone else, it may fall through later on, so why unnecessarily worry them so, yes, that's common in the industry.

"They dispute this was told to her. It's a little unclear whether they dispute that, but is this something Ms. Foote could have come up on her own? She is constructing a case against him where here is what he told me, it's an insurance guy. She happens on a very common lie that Mr. Hill or his companies, and apparently the industry, might have told to a lot of people.

"Does that have the ring of truth? I don't know. But it was a lie. Mr. Hill admits it was a lie, and if you think about it, if Mr. Hill had told her on September 13th we have got a national tenant moving in, we are going to be moving you out, why would they lie? I mean he has already caused the anxiety that would have been caused when it's being told there is a national tenant coming in. He says, gosh, I told her on September 13th so there would be no reason to lie, and in this case and pursuant to the instructions that Judge Sparr will give you, you need to use the common sense. That's the real beauty of a jury; they apply the common sense to what is a more likely scenario happening. And I want to impress that actions speak a lot louder than words here. They wouldn't have to lie if they had already told her she was being kicked out of that space.

"So the evidence was then that once Ms. Foote saw the insurance guy and they said hey, we are trying to reduce the insurance rates, she thought it was for the whole shopping center. She says in passing to the guy, my gosh, you have been here for four or five hours in my little store, it's going to take you an awful long time to do the whole shopping center, isn't it, and he says the whole shopping center? I am just doing your store. And that's a distressing thing to find out, and particularly when you have been told not to worry, just an insurance thing, pay no attention.

"And her testimony is she called Dan Hill and he wrapped it up and stayed out of it, but Ms. Foote is a smart cookie, she knows something is wrong and she calls a lawyer she knows who has done some work for her on other business things. That's Phil Pankoff. He has been a lawyer in the Denver community for over 30 years. He told her, he testified, I will find out what's going on for you. He puts in a phone call to Dan Hill and talks to him on September 26th. That's undisputed as well. And at that time Dan Hill says well, it's because a tenant is coming in and we had to make measurements.

"At that time not a single word was said about relocating Ms. Foote. It's just that she is out of there. Not that they are going to relocate. Now that's disputed testimony. Mr. Hill says Mr. Hill says I started telling her on the 13th and, in fact, Mr. Pankoff called me to tell me that we were relocating. You might recall Mr. Hill's testimony that he said Pankoff called and said hello, this is Phil Pankoff, you are moving her, aren't you, and you are measuring for the new tenant, good-bye. And Mr. Pankoff's testimony was exactly contrary to that; what's going on, why are you doing this, you are moving her, somebody else is moving in, no discussion about relocation, good-bye. And Mr. Pankoff calls Ms. Foote, and for the first time in her life she understands that her space has been rented.

"Now this case isn't just about her space being rented, but up to this point we can see a definite pattern of secrecy in the negotiation and deception to Ms. Foote when she had a right to know what they were doing, and I think that just helps you assess the credibility and analyze the evidence. That's the lens that you are going to study the rest of the evidence through. You might believe that Mr. Pankoff didn't get it either, that there was this discussion Mr. Hill testified about relocating and Mr. Pankoff, who has been a lawyer for 30-plus years, didn't understand that's what he was saying. That's what you have to believe, in fact, if you are going to believe Mr. Hill's testimony on this point because Mr. Hill said he made the point.

"What other evidence do we have then to assess the credibility and assess the facts? Well, one of them is the e-mails that the Yarmouth Group and the Tabor Center, the defendants, sent back and forth between themselves chattering about the GNC developments and what they were going to do with Africa House. You might recall in Plaintiff's Exhibit 5 there was a series of three e-mails, and the first e-mail was from Dee Torres talking to Dan Hill saying hi, Dan, I want to know the procedure. Do I inform Africa House, or do you take the papers up to them and tell them that they are leaving—they are leaving. And then she wonders, in parentheses, could it be that easy. Is it that easy to get somebody out of here. Mr. Hill sends an e-mail back; I am the one who handles it and I will do it 30 days before or after the GNC deal is completed, so he is saying what his time frame is to notify them for the termination. And then Ms. Torres sends back an e-mail to that saying I have had Phil look at the lease, and the kickout requires only 15 days. I have just saved us 30 days. We can kick her out quicker than we originally thought.

"Now I suppose if you are stretching it and bending over backwards you could think the kickout doesn't mean kickout, it just means move down the hall, but she didn't use that term and, in fact, the next point is these are very specific terms. These are real estate professionals. They do this all the time. You don't use loose terms in contracts and leases, and they were talking about what the clause for termination in the lease was. And the lease analysis sort of puts one of the final nails in the coffin on this point.

"I have—I will get it—it's the blow-up of the lease that Ms. Foote was operating under, and it's Joint Exhibit 13 when you get the exhibits to deliberate, but the last page is the signature page of the 1993 lease, and Section 16 governs what a landlord can do in regard to relocating or terminating a tenant's stay at the Tabor Center, and it says that if the landlord in its sole discretion requires the premises at any time during the term, landlord may relocate tenant to any available space in the Tabor Center or terminate this lease.

"Those are two separate things. I asked Mr. Hill if those are two separate things. I asked Ms. Torres, and they clearly are. I mean we all can read that. You may relocate or they can terminate. And they chose to terminate. And is there any evidence to support the proposition, which I am suggesting, that if they meant to tell her that they would relocate her, is really what they were saying they *wanted* to relocate her? Well, there is. I mean we had a couple of exhibits that we put in that proves really beyond the shadow of a doubt, as they say on TV, that when they want to relocate they know how to do it.

"There was a notice of termination given to the Candy Barrel, which is a separate business. There was a notice of termination given to One Hour Photo shop, which was a separate business, and that says we hereby elect to terminate your lease. Next paragraph, if you would like to relocate, please contact me at your convenience, or even pursuant to our previous discussions we will relocate you, just give me a call. But that was conspicuously absent in the very legally typed esteemed notice of termination that they sent on October 14th to Ms. Foote. And, in fact, an analysis of that termination, that's Joint Exhibit 4 which you will see in the jury room when you deliberate. Joint Exhibit 4 is single paragraph, we hereby terminate your lease.

"You may recall it is legally intimidating, frankly. It's served on her five different ways, if you believe the testimony. One is served by certified mail. Second, it's hand-delivered to her premises at the store, but if that wasn't good enough, it was mailed to her premises to the store. If that wasn't good enough they mailed it to an old defunct address on Third Avenue. They knew she wasn't there anymore, but they are crossing their legal T's and dotting their legal I's. And, third, if you believe Mr. Hill, he also verbally told her they were terminating. That's covering your legal bases, and isn't it a coincidence, if you think about it, that everything in this case about terminating her is in writing and legally secure and solid, and everything about relocation is coincidental and orally and yeah, we did it, but no, we didn't extend it to her in writing. It's not really consistent with the way they act, as

Ms. Foote's testimony, that's because it didn't happen that way.

"Actions speak louder. Ms. Foote testified that at the time she was terminated on October 14th, there were no pending offers of putting her anywhere else, and you are looking right down the face of the Christmas season, which is a huge part of the retail season. Frankly, that's undisputed. They don't say there were any offers for space as of the time they terminated it, so imagine her response when she gets the notice of termination that says you have 15 days to skedaddle and there is no suggestion of where she will land in the Center. She urgently sought space in other shopping centers. She hired not one, but two brokers to help her find space, and one of them even talked to the Tabor Center to no avail because there was no offer on the space there, but they both looked outside of the Tabor Center urgently to find her space, and that's because everybody knew she was being evicted. Everybody also knew, by the way, and it's undisputed, that she wanted to stay in the Tabor Center.

"Now what rational woman or man or anybody would say I really want to stay here and they are saying we really want you to stay here, but they are urgently looking in Writer's Square or Lodo where, it just wasn't the case, and if you really want a piece of evidence that drives this point home solidly, take a look at Joint Exhibit 6, Pat McHenry who was the witness called by them was one of the brokers that Tseghe retained to help her find space.

And Ms. McHenry, a very experienced broker, says I was looking for a long-term place for her store to land because she needed a space. It was October 16th at that time, two days after she gets the notice of termination, and Pat McHenry said these types of negotiations for a four-year lease like this typically [take] three months. You might remember her testimony, sometimes they take up to a year. It's a very, very laborious process. But in this case Joint Exhibit 6 reflects an October 16th letter that says we need a long-term space and we must take occupancy by October 25th, which is nine nights, which is not three months or nine months or seven months. This is our generalities. We need it now.

"And that is inferential, strong, strong, inferential support for Ms. Foote, and it rejects, on the actions speak louder theory, the defendant's position on this. It is undisputed, by the way, that Ms. Foote wanted to leave. There is no evidence from Mr. Hill or Ms. Torres or somebody that hey, I wanted to leave, she wanted to stay, and she was able to communicate that to them and she did. The efforts to relocate that the defendants take solace in, basically the one they argue the most, is in the Fleet Feet space, and that turns out to be October 18th, this is after the notice of termination, she put it in writing, you can stay in Fleet Feet but only until October 28th, 1997. That's the only one that is really put in writing.

"But let's explore what they were saying about the Fleet Feet space. Very early on in September, at the September 30th meeting, she had found out that the national tenant was taking her space, she started looking for alternative [spaces], okay, where can I be. And Mr. Hill suggested at that time 202, that's the Fleet Feet space. Maybe I can get you a one-year lease there, and I hope you recall Ms. Foote's testimony which was back on Monday or Tuesday, which said that made me feel better. If I could get one-year lease on the Fleet Feet space maybe I can sell some of my inventory. Remember, she had just gotten a huge inventory from Africa, she had taken out a huge $100,000 loan on her place. So Mr. Hill checked into whether this one-year lease was available option. Mr. Hill admitted that on the stand.

"This is the area that Mr. Grunschlag on his opening mischaracterized, frankly. He said they were talking about a one-year lease in Fleet Feet and Tseghe Foote was not interested. Well, that's not true. That wasn't what the evidence showed. She was very interested in that space. Why did that space get taken away from her? Mr. Hill, after several days had passed, no, that won't do, somebody else is looking into that space, so that one is out, that won't work. So that was by October 1st or September 30th or something like that.

"So again, uncertain, and occasionally they would dangle the possibility of space 202, which was a workable space, it was too big, but a workable one and certainly better than the alternative, but this was the guy that was wishy-washy. He couldn't decide if he was going to move out during the Christmas season or when it was going to be, so the lease to the Africa House was conditioned on two things; one, we don't know if it happens, and, two, if you do get it, don't think you will be staying more than four months, which is ultimately what they put in writing. Her business is an established, solid business. It can't be changing places every three or four months.

"There was on the 14th, the day of the eviction notice, I asked Mr. Hill why didn't you put just like you did all those other letters, let's relocate or talk about relocation. I invite you to do that, and he said the reason we don't, there are ongoing discussions, but that's not true is it?

"The last piece of evidence we have about discussions regarding what space she might be in is the October 14th meeting where Mr. Schwartz is present and Mr. Hill and Ms. Foote, and that's the one Dee Torres showed up by conference call. There weren't ongoing discussions. Ms. Foote was left dangling, and that was unpunctuated, there is no more uncertainty, here is your termination notice, and no invitation to relocate.

"Well, again actions speak louder than words. If they were really relocating her, Ms. Foote would have explored that, but she was really forced to hire legal counsel, and she hired specialized legal counsel, a man who specialized not only in civil rights law, but has also a significant background in landlord/tenant disputes, and he started on her behalf to work this problem. That was David Fine. He testified on Thursday. He became involved, and his testimony to you was Tabor Center was not interested in relocating her. They had no intention to relocate her. Maybe out of an abundance of caution, I said, Mr. Fine, are you sure, and he said absolutely. No intention whatsoever.

"Now it's conceivable to me that, like Mr. Pankoff, Mr. Fine just didn't understand that when they told him we are relocating her, what's the big deal, of course we are relocating her, but Mr. Fine said that's not what he understood, and he is 100 percent clear on it. So clear, in fact, that he took a remarkable step. He filed an emergency court action to stop the eviction. Now do you think an attorney would do that, come to court and say we have to stop the eviction in the face of the quite obvious response from the defendants who had come in and said, your Honor, we are not evicting them, we are relocating her, we have told her a thousand times we are relocating her. Of course not. He filed that because they were kicking her out even though they deny that now. He said they had absolutely no interest in relocating her, and this is an extraordinary legal action.

"Most cases get filed and come to court a year or two later. He got into court or had a hearing set that week. At the last hour, he says, literally the last hour, the night before the court hearing, finally, finally he accomplished a concession from Tabor Center saying she can stay if you don't go to court right now. Stop the processes and we will let her stay, and then we will let it go until the jury or the case is over. And only then, after significant hard work and going through extraordinary steps, did he accomplish keeping her in the Center. And Tabor Center and the defendants say we were keeping her in the Center the whole time. Mr. Fine's testimony was not rebutted in the least.

"Additional evidence that Ms. Foote was treated differently, and we suggest because of her race, and that's what this case is about, and because of her race, by the way, means that her race was a factor. The Judge will instruct you in the legal instructions; that doesn't have to be the only reason, and it doesn't even have to be the primary or dominant reason. If her race made a difference, if it was a motivating factor, not the only one or even the biggest one, then you would find in favor of Ms. Foote on her discrimination claims.

"So how do you figure that out beyond showing their case makes no sense? You could compare her to the treatment of other tenants. It's undisputed that Tabor Center has huge vacancies. I mean this was a struggling retail center. Fifty-six percent vacancy rate, or 56 percent, maybe, was filled up at the start of 1996. Those reports are in evidence and there has been testimony about it. There is not a whit of evidence from the defendants that they kicked anybody else out of the Center ever. They terminated a couple of leases, and in the same breath relocated them down the hall and, frankly, as they said in their opening statement, and I don't think they have changed now, there is not a single legitimate business reason—legitimate business reason—which would allow them to kick her out of the Center, which would want them to kick her out of the Center, so we have to look at what reason then that is that—would that be.

"Well, ask yourselves, I think, and talk about it in the deliberations, how did they treat other tenants? I think the evidence fairly shows a picture of bending over backwards to keep other tenants, as you might expect. I mean this is a struggling center. You want to jump in. You don't want to pay rent if you don't have to pay rent. If you have that obligation that's too burdensome we will make it a percentage deal instead of a minimum rent. You don't want to pay the side charges, you don't have to pay them.

"The example of American Baseball Classic, they couldn't make it on long-term lease; they were failing. Did they get kicked out? Heck no. They cut them a deal. They cut them a great deal actually. Seven percent sales. I mean that's just sweetheart, but this doesn't get out—this was after Ms. Foote had already filed her claim. In order for this not to get out, they said you must keep this secret. If this gets out this isn't a deal anymore. But that was a very nice thing to do for a tenant that they didn't do for Ms. Foote. She didn't need it, by the way. She needed no rent concession.

"FT Casuals was a store over 3,000 square feet. Their annual sales were far less than what

Ms. Foote had in half the space. The testimony, I think brought out from Mr. Hill, was that their rent-to-sales ratio, the statistic which is supposed to govern the retail world, far exceeded 20 percent. This was a company that they decided to keep on the premises as well.

"CB Traditions, you've got to want to be the owner of CB Traditions. These guys had the greatest deal. This is a long-term lease, 1989 to 1994, which is in large part the previous owners, which might be a good excuse, except it was extended three times by Yarmouth Group on long-term bases. One of those for 25 months. They had 10 percent—every dollar you make send us ten cents, so that's a great deal because if you don't make but $100 in a month, your rent that month is $10. And your rent-to-sales ratio, by the way, that will always be 10 percent which, according to all the experts and everybody else's testimony, is just a shining example of a good business. If you have 10 percent rent-to-sales ratio. That's why the rent-to-sales ratio is a fallacy.

"You have to look at all the facts, not just rent-to-sales ratio. Mountain Man was another example. I won't go through them all, but the Mountain Man was an example, based upon six months' sales experience in the Tabor Center, six months, they said let's offer her a long-term lease, and they offered her a lease that most certainly would have put her above 20 percent in the rent-to-sales ratio. They were trying to have her pay 72 bucks a square foot for her space, and based upon her sales, the owner of that business, who knows her sales, says my rent-to-sales ratio would have been above 20 percent. She negotiated some of that. The negotiations ultimately failed. She ultimately negotiated downward, but Tabor Center extended that offer, and they were prepared to live with it, and if Mountain Man accepts it, that rent-to-sales ratio is additional—it's over 20 percent, and it was terrible if you believe all of their evidence.

"So that's how they treated other tenants. And Ms. Foote was just seeking fair treatment. She wanted some long-term security. She wanted a long-term lease, and we will talk about her qualifications in a moment about that, but even on a short-term—so-called short-term lease, you can plan for the future if you are a business owner as long as they don't kick you out improperly, and that's in fact what Ms. Foote had done since 1992.

"In this case she said she testified, and there is no rebuttal of this, and it certainly makes sense, that once they began these actions and this case started, I couldn't plan for the future. How could I invest in my business knowing at any minute I can be kicked out of here? How could I expect to grow and hope to do all of these things I have in the plans, advertising, sent out brochures, she was going to talk about catalog sales, those sorts of things, all get put on hold when they tell her they don't want her in, and that's what any rational businesswoman would do, and there was a stipulation right on the eve of the court hearing we are talking about, but when this case is over she still doesn't know what would happen to her. Boom, she may be out on the street the next day. Whether or not this is legal action is still an open question.

"So was she a worthy tenant at Tabor Center? Well, the defendants I think have pulled a tricky one here. All of their witnesses have testified about the GNC lease and that Africa House has been able to meet the lease entered into by GNC, but that is certainly not the universe of options presented to either Africa House or to the Tabor Center in this case. Like I say, don't be fooled into thinking we are saying we absolutely had a right to 322, to that unit; she just wanted to operate her business in the Center which is where her customers [knew] Africa House was.

"There were many, many long-term tenants in the Tabor Center that didn't meet the requirements of the GNC lease. Likewise, there are many, many leases at the Tabor Center that aren't as strict or as high as the GNC lease. So I think it's misleading to say she can't meet the GNC lease, therefore she is not qualified for tenancy at the [Tabor Center]. Of course there are other options. The candid witness testimony was that these leases are negotiated on a case-by-case basis. You make concessions, there is give and take, and that could have happened with Africa House as well.

"She is not required to say how did GNC negotiate, they did pretty well, okay, that's the terms I will like as well. And, in fact, are there examples of that? Of course there are examples of that. Africa House's sales per square foot, for example, were superior to Brooks Brothers sales per square foot. That was testimony that was admitted to by Mr. Ehrlich. Brooks Brothers is pretty impressive, glamorous tenant, but they didn't do as good as Africa House at Tabor Center. Certainly Eagle's Nest, that's a national tenant. Their sales were inferior to Africa House's.

"We heard testimony this morning from Tim Gonerka, their expert, that says GNC was at Tabor Center in 1990, their sales were so low that's why they left. Of course that wasn't even looked into by the leasing people at the Tabor Center. They didn't apparently have that type of institutional history to know that, and they went in and got GNC—by the way, there is not a single shred of evidence about how GNC is doing, about whether they are selling that $800,000 that Dee Torres says nationally. But how they are doing is a mystery. It is not in evidence, although those statistics certainly exist.

"And an important point, I think, in considering the qualifications of Africa House is sales potential. Their expert witness, Tim Gonerka, says a responsible, experienced manager will look at sales potential, not sales, sales potential, and the evidence in this case before you on the sales potential of Africa House is impressive. She had built her business for really eight or nine years but really four or five at the Tabor Center, and she built a strong customer base. She built committed customers, good-quality merchandise, she had developed to the next level really where she got a lot of working capital, $100,000, and excellent inventory, and she was just ready to take off at the time that these events happened.

"And two witnesses, Andy Warren, who is a professional small business consultant, testified that he analyzed her operation and the inventory and everything she was doing, and she was not only on the right track, but with just a modicum of advertising, if she reaches out to something other than word of mouth with advertising she could double her sales conservatively. Now he may have been selling her services to help her do that, but he also looked into it, and there wasn't any impeachment of his professional ability to make such an assessment. I mean he looked through everything and said she could be making $80,000 or $40,000 a month, and she was making about twenty at the time. Forty-thousand dollars a month is $480,000 a year. That was what he testified to.

"Lew Gaiter also testified for you. He is also a small business consultant, and he was even more optimistic. He said with a few business moves she could increase her sales 3 to 400 percent, triple or quadruple her sales. So Mr. Gaiter is the one that talked about catalog sales, and Mr. Warren and Mr. Gaiter also talked about advertising. Those were things she could have done for those who didn't know about the existence of Africa

House and, of course, that's what advertising is about, and, of course, that increases sales. They . . . didn't bring anybody to suggest otherwise, and they didn't cross-examine them to challenge their testimony in any way.

"So there was an untapped fertile market for her merchandise, and they had grown strong and they were strong. Mr. Hill admits her sales were going up. And what evidence do we have she was doing well? This is a young woman who was setting up a business on her own and was working to build it and was doing pretty well. She paid off the mortgage of her house, too—and then that secured the $100,000 loan. Not many people I know of her age and experience and business [sense] are able to pay off the mortgage of [a] . . . house.

"Her business is doing well, she is using the proceeds to meet her personal and business obligations, and she has always met every business obligation that she . . . undertook. But Mr. Grunschlag in his opening said this is a struggling business; in fact, she was losing money, and their evidence that she was losing money were the tax returns that said she suffered a loss. As the tax return shows, she suffered a loss of $7,000 or $10,000 in a particular year.

"Hopefully the jury will bring its life experience to the table in deliberations and know that tax returns certainly don't tell the whole story of a successful business or not. I was surprised in college to learn in the economics class that U.S.

Steel, one of the biggest companies in the world, really, continually suffered losses, and they seemed to be making a lot of money otherwise and their executives do too. If the tax return is all the evidence they have that she doesn't know how to run a business, then I think that falls short of the mark.

"On this rent-to-sales ratio point, just so I can finish up the statistics and her qualifications, a couple of things need to be said. One of the experts and the people that run the case, the people that were on the scene, Dee Torres and Dan Hill, said if you have a 15 percent rent-to-sales ratio or more you are doomed to failure. It's [an] almost certainty to go out of business too. Mr. Gonerka said that too. But Dee Torres unequivocally said it's usually 17 or 18 percent, but for a store like Africa House it's 15 percent.

"Second point on that was Mr. Hill candidly admitted the way the lease was structured for Africa House, it was mathematically impossible for her to beat that standard. No matter, what she had to pay 15 percent of her sales to rent. That's what her lease says. She had a base, but that was determined by the 15 percent number and a break point, and anything above that was 15 percent number. So she could have made a million dollars. That's what Mr. Hill agreed to, and if you just looked at that statistic, this is a troubled business certain to go down the tubes, which is, of course, ridiculous. And it is ridiculous, and I think even on a good day all of them would admit just looking at that statistic is wrong and it is misleading. There were several stores that have a rent-to-sales ratio exceeding 15 percent. Hers, by the way, couldn't go below 15 percent, but she is operating it efficiently. It was exactly 15 percent. Her sales could go above 15 percent. If her sales were very low she would have to pay the minimum base rent which would send her statistics up. But she always kept it at the lowest minimum mathematical possibilities.

"So what about the statistical initials, sales per square foot, rent-to-sales ratio. It's a case they put on afterwards. This wasn't something they were considering when they said Africa House had to go; this was something they had to come up with after they were sued and she stood up to them. You have to come up with a defense; let's dazzle them with these numbers and they bring in experts. Nobody testified that these were the things they were considering ahead of time. The best they can do on that is in this October 1st conference call, Dee Torres said she pulled out a sales report and started punching in numbers and came up with 37 percent, but by that time they made the decision that Africa House had to go, so even then this is an after-the-fact sort of excuse, justification to treat Africa House the way they did.

"It's sort of like an employer coming in and saying I don't think this is a job for a black person so you are fired, and the black person surprisingly says you can't do that, I am going to sue you, and then they go back and think about it and say okay, well, it was because you were late three times last month then. That wouldn't do the trick. Anybody can come up with an excuse. The law calls that a pretext, not the truth. It's a reason they have come up with to cover up the reason that really motivated them, and in this case that's exactly what the defendants have done.

"And why would they try to get rid of Ms. Foote? I mean she has been successful at every venture she has tried against the odds really. An Ethiopian immigrant setting up her own business in a major United States city, against all of the odds. Every place she has been she has met all of her financial obligations both personally and business-wise, and who are they to say she can't pay more. She has cleared the bar every time they set it, and she clears it more and they raise it and she clears it more. I used to try a high jump in grade school and you don't need to clear the bar by a hundred yards. And they are saying you aren't clearing it by very much, you can't play anymore.

"But let's analyze the evidence of what they said because actions do speak louder than words, but sometimes words that slip out speak volumes, and we have got that in this case, and I have got to tell you evidence like this doesn't come along every day in these discrimination cases. They made several statements which give us a window into their motivation. For example, a walk-through, early 1996, an entourage that includes probably three or four people, but we know that Dan Hill and Karl

Ehrlich are included, and this is right at the outset of the management team taking over, the new management team at Yarmouth. The earliest walk-through that Dan Hill can remember with the executives like this. And they come to Africa House, and the testimony is Karl Ehrlich says this has to go, and I told you in opening statement this was the statement made, and Mr. Hill, while initially trying to testify that he said this sign has to go, finally admitted that he didn't say this sign has to go, that's just what Mr. Hill was hearing, that's what he thought he meant. But the statement was, "This has to go." So we have an arguably ambiguous statement. There is, it's innocent; oh, it's a bad sign; it needs to be—Ehrlich even said I think it needs to be lighted, but that was demonstrably wrong because she was a short-term tenant. That's a long-term tenants's obligation so he doesn't adequately explain it. Mr. Hill said I think he meant this sign has to go. Why didn't they tell her about it? Your guess is as good as mine. If the sign has to go, you would think maybe they would tell the owner of the store that maybe the sign has to go.

"What does this statement mean? Well, let's look at it in context. The only reason we know about the statement, the only reason you know about the statement, is because Dan Hill told Tseghe Foote about the statement. And Tseghe was able to testify to it. And when did Dan Hill tell Ms. Foote that this statement was made? In September of 1996. This is months after the event, and the context of this meeting is Ms. Foote goes to him and says why, why aren't you offering me security here. Why are you ignoring me. And in that context he says, let me tell you a story. And proceeds to tell her—and this is at the September 30th meeting—proceeds to tell her about the walk-through months earlier with Mr. Ehrlich.

"Now if their story is true, that we are just talking about the sign, then he is on a different planet than she is because she is saying why aren't you offering the security and why are you kicking me out basically, and he starts talking about a sign from months ago. That makes no sense. What makes sense is Ms. Foote's story which is he is answering her question. Why are you treating me this way. Well, let me tell you a story. We had a walk-through, and it's not me, it's my boss, and I am a new worker here, right? I only started a few months ago, and my boss and I are going by, my boss says this has to go, that's your answer. And while credit is due to Mr. Hill for being honest in that conversation with Ms. Foote, all of that credit is taken away for not being honest in testifying about what that statement meant in this Court. It's preposterous to believe that they are talking about that sign has to go. It's preposterous.

"When Mr. Ehrlich testified he tried to tie it to some sort of idea of her numbers, but Mr. Ehrlich hadn't poured over her numbers, wasn't looking at it; they were walking along and says this has to go. They weren't looking for a space for GNC either.

GNC expressed an interest in the summer of 1996. It was just this has to go. It wasn't this has to go next door; the statement was, "This has to go." You have to evaluate that.

"Frankly Mr. Ehrlich described Africa House after a little prodding, and I had to ask several questions, but he admitted he in the past described Africa House as an unsophisticated tenant; that's another euphemism. And I said what do you mean, Mr. Ehrlich, an unsophisticated tenant, and he put it in a report, unsophisticated tenants with short-term leases, he said when I said unsophisticated tenant I meant they had a short-term lease which really again really, really begs credibility.

"And finally the context of "this has to go" was at that September 30th meeting was the follow-up on whether space 202 was going to work on the 26th or 27th after Ms. Foote had said what do you mean there is another tenant, and they started talking about 202. That's when Mr. Hill said I will look into the possibility of a one-year lease at 202 for you, so the September 30th meeting was the result of his looking into it. He said let me tell you this story. And this has to go. That's why 202 wasn't available. It wasn't 202 or 203. It's you are devaluing the property, which is another—your store devalues the property, which is another face and another statement that Mr. Hill made which we will talk about in a moment.

"Mr. Hill denies using the phrase "this devalues the property." I asked him, you said that, didn't you, and he said no, I don't think I ever used that phrase, devalue property, and he was pretty strong on his denial, but about five follow-up questions it's clear he believed so. I asked him, what is it about the name that bothers you, and he said it decreases the sales, the better name would give it better sales and, second, our point here is to maximize the value of the property and higher sales maximize this property, so the name which decreases sales, which is one of those simple mathematical axioms that I can't remember the name of it from high school, but if A equals B, and B equals C, then A and B equals C. If he devalues the property, then he certainly believes that the name Africa House or the store devalues the property.

"You would have to believe that Ms. Foote is profoundly lying or again not processing information correctly to believe otherwise. She says he tells me that it devalues the property. In the same conversation that September 30th, the same conversation where she heard, "This has to go." Now interestingly, you heard a witness this morning, Louise Selzer, testify—they called her to testify, and she talked a little bit about what the name might be, but they didn't ask her about all of the other evidence which has been adduced at this trial from that September 30th meeting such as did he say devalue the property. Did he say, "This has to go?" She was a witness at most of that meeting, but they decided not to elicit that testimony, and if they wanted to deny it and they had an eye witness deny it don't you think they would have had her deny it?

"It brings us to one of these other potentially ambiguous—and these add up—but potentially ambiguous statements, why don't you change the name of your store. This ends up going full circle, and I don't think their story holds up under scrutiny on this either. The evidence is at various times Mr. Ehrlich and Mr. Hill and Ms. Torres all suggested that the name of the store was not very good or it could be improved if they threw museum or store or something in there instead of "house," and when pressed on cross-examination each of them say the name Africa House doesn't sound very good, and it's "house" that bothers them. And Ms. Torres said it wasn't glamorous. She didn't remember saying that, but Mr. Hill did remember that she said that. He testified when he called him as a witness, and then she testified she didn't remember saying that, and the very next witness was Dan Hill. They brought him up on the stand for another point, but she didn't have him say no, he didn't say that. But they conceded this isn't a glamorous name, and the word "house" somehow makes it an inferior name.

"Now am I missing something here? Is that even on its face credible that Africa House is a bad name that reflects inferior products rather than high-end products? I think it just falls upon the statement. But Ms. Selzer, I think, gave the best credible evidence. Africa House is a great name, I don't think it devalues or sounds cheap or something like that. You each could exchange your own opinion on that, but if you come up with really good reasons why "house" is a bad name for it, send me an anonymous letter or something why that is a bad name. It doesn't make sense. In fact, the real story, Ms. Foote's testimony, is they thought Africa House devalued the property; not the name Africa "House" but "Africa" House.

"There is testimony which is now conflicting regarding Ms. Torres' belief that this store wasn't glamorous. She doesn't remember doing that. You heard an independent third-party witness, Jana Thorpe, talk about negotiations that she engaged in for a long-term lease. She was the lady who runs the Mountain Man Nut and Fruit store. And she was asking who the other long-term tenants were going to be, and when it came to Africa House she testified—and she has got no dog in this fight, she is an independent third-party witness—she testified that Dee Torres told her, oh, no, no, no, no, Africa House doesn't fit into the image of the Tabor Center. They won't be long-term. And they brought Ms. Torres up there now to say I didn't say that, and that is credibility determination. She denied it. And one of those two people is telling the truth and one of them is not. Ms. Thorpe, though, understood it immediately when she heard it that she was saying Africa House has a black owner selling African-oriented goods, and black customers. She heard it very clearly in her mind as a racial comment. That was her testimony and it's sworn testimony.

"So, that's, I think, a lot of the evidence on what's called the liability side, which side is going to win and which side is going to lose. We will talk some about damages in a moment, but I want to talk about just generally what their defense, their economics. We are just doing business here and take no offense, ma'am, you just weren't worthy enough economically to be here. Well, Mr. Grunschlag four times—I counted them—four times on opening statement admitted that there is not a legitimate business reason to want Africa House out of the Center, and that's important legally. There is—and it's undisputed—they say it, we say it too, there is not a legitimate business reason to have Africa House out of the Center.

"They have tried to, as I mentioned earlier at the top of this closing argument, they have tried to divert the focus onto unit 322, and that's sort of like look over there, but that's not what the case is about. We are talking about staying in the Center. And I just note I think that discrimination, when race is taken into account in making an adverse decision such as a decision to terminate a lease, these days it's different maybe than it was 50 years ago. It's not—we don't see discrimination in the sense of a bull horn or spraying blacks with the fire hose, something as obvious and demonstrably wrong I think that would turn all our stomachs, and it doesn't happen particularly in Colorado anymore.

"That's—there are exceptions, but that's not the way it happens anymore, but it's true and subtle and illegal. It happens in the scenario of less respect being paid to one person versus another, less attention being given in the context of a shopping mall or employment setting or something, it really happens in the lack of equal opportunity.

"If any of that is based upon race it is illegal, and Judge Sparr will instruct you as much when he reads you the charge. Economics, which is their flag they send up the pole saying this is a defense, is not a defense to discrimination. Economics, it's not okay to discriminate because, I asked one of their witnesses, the high-level executive Karl Ehrlich, don't be fooled, this is race not economics because a lot of race discrimination in our history has been tagged with an economic justification; we do it because of economics, people might not hire people based on their race in public contact positions because maybe they would lose customers, that doesn't make it okay.

"Our civil rights laws passed really right after the Civil War for starters, and that will be the ones presented to you in instructions, present just that very argument. You can move out a tenant who has a month-to-month lease. They don't have ten-year security. We aren't saying they had an automatic right. There is not a lot of built-in security to month-to-month lease. You can do it virtually for the thinnest of reasons, but if it ever becomes infected with race that's an illegal reason, that's not one you could use. So if they decided they would make the top floor entirely a Food Court, then that would have been good enough and she would have been out of luck, but if race enters into the equation they lose and the instructions on this will be very important. Again race needs to be a motivating factor, not the only one, and at that point they would have violated Ms. Foote's and Africa House's rights. And if you find that then you turn to remedy.

"How do you remedy this illegal conduct? Well, a jury is given—as I think I mentioned in opening statement—a fairly limited selection of choices. You can give damages. Monetary awards is all a jury can give, and in this case there are two types of damages that the jury will be asked to award. One is called compensatory damages and one is called punitive damages. They are different purposes. They have different methods of calculation.

"I will talk about compensatory damages first, and compensatory damages is really two types. One is economic loss and one is noneconomic loss. On economic loss there is really two ways to look at this. You heard testimony from Dr. Kaempfer, which was somewhat tortured I will concede, but the amounts he came up with were legitimate and quite plausible really that the move that she was required to undergo caused a consequence of $75,000. That's moving from the third floor to the second floor. And you can certainly award that amount. You should award that amount. That's at a minimum what she suffered in real life, but more importantly than that is the damages from what they did to her business.

"And those are far more significant what they did when they tried to evict Ms. Foote in October of 1996, was put the skids on her business plan. She testified unrefuted, and I don't know how they could, that she was right at the threshold of the next level. She had secured this inventory. She had business working capital. And she was about to reach her American dream. She even has big dreams, maybe not reachable, I don't know if they are reachable or not, I wouldn't bet against her, though, but her plans were she has multiple stores maybe moving into other states, maybe franchises, I don't know.

"But they were trying to kick her out, and I hope you find it's illegal, but at that point, as Ms. Foote testified from the stand, she couldn't do anything proactive for her business. She couldn't invest in her business. You wouldn't go and get more inventory and, indeed, she did not. She has taken no trips to Africa since these events have happened. She put the complete skids on any plans too advertise or do catalog sales because she has no certainty as to how this will turn out. She had to stop and tread water for the last two-and-a-half years since this has happened. And that's what happened; she has treaded water economically. She was building a solid customer base, and she just has leveled off because it's a holding pattern. That's what's happening.

"But what might she have done? There is not speculation, there is evidence to base these. We all sometimes have to conclude what might happen tomorrow, and that's not necessarily speculation if there is good basis for it, and in this case both Mr. Warren and Mr. Gaiter testified she could have increased her sales quickly, relatively quickly, for a business because she was that type of business that was just ready to take off.

"Mr. Warren said she could have made $40,000 a month. Mr. Gaiter said 3 to 400 percent increase in sales. Well, what does that translate into? She is making $250,000 a year in her old space. It was $22,000 in 1996, but that doesn't include the last two months since she got moved, so the expert witness Gonerka this morning said that was a fair projection; she might have made $250,000. It was actually higher than that. And if you took the most conservative of the testimony, Mr. Warren's testimony, she could have doubled that if she had continued on with her plans as she was, then she could have made $500,000 a year in sales, and there was a stipulation entered into during Dr. Kaempfer's testimony that it's a fair projection everybody was on notice that damages might be claimed for three years, and three years at a loss of sales of $250,000 a year is $750,000 in lost sales.

"This is truly the cost of having to put the skids on and stop and say I am not going to do anything. And actions again speak louder than words. She really did put the skids on. She was terrified by the insecurity that was being inflicted on her. She paid back the $100,000 working capital. Because she had to batten down the hatches, probably a phrase Tseghe never used, but descriptive, and said I have to weather the storm, and that's the economic loss that happened to her and three years of losses of $750,000.

"But—and I mentioned this in opening statement—I think that more significant damage component on the compensatory damages side is not the economic loss, even though that's significant. If you lose money that should not be ignored, certainly. That's an important thing and it can be awarded and made up by an award of money in a verdict. But the other part of compensatory damages under our system of law is somewhat clumsy. It allows the jury to award a remedy for things such as the emotional trauma, the effect, the impacts of this on Ms. Foote personally. What did this do to her as a person. And what did this do to her business.

"And in this case it's difficult, isn't it, to distinguish between Tseghe Foote and Africa House. Africa House is her very identity. It's—in fact, there was some testimony from one of the witnesses that he kept getting the same name of the store wrong. The name of the store was immaterial to him. He called her the Africa store and Africa lady one time. She is Africa House, that is Tseghe Foote, and she was building what she had wanted to build since age 14 and had the courage and fortitude not only to build it in the first place, which I think we would all agree is impressive, but the courage and the fortitude to fight for it when it's threatened, which is why we are here.

"Fighting for her American dream is what she was doing, and she wanted me to say that in closing because that is the way she sees this, and it's something we learn about in 8th grade, maybe in civics, and these are important principles, but sometimes we close the book and move on and sometimes, unfortunately, just enter the world of economics, and the ideas and principles we learned about in civics are sort of left to rust, but she still lives to do them, and that's what her story was, and maybe anything more than any of us can think about her business and herself are very closely tied. They are an identity.

"And despite having doors slammed in her face, probably not even an uncommon experience for her in her life, nothing was handed to her. She fought on. And in this case, for purposes of compensatory damages, the jury needs to use its collective judgment and wisdom to figure out what something like that is worth. And in this case she was handed the worst sort of indignity. They are telling Ms. Foote, who is Africa House, who is Ms. Foote, that your store, the value of your store, is inadequate. You are not valuable. And that is the message that they sent, maybe not even realizing the impact of it, but it's the unmistakable message that they are telling her. And her identity, which is proud and professional and undeniably black, it's not a coincidence that an African-American is selling African merchandise.

"Her identity, which is respectful and respected and hard-working and dignified, was at once disposed of with this condescending flip of the hand that we can do better than you. You are not worthy to be here. What level of money can compensate for that? Well, no amount really. I don't know the answer to that. There is no tricky formula, lost wages or fixing the bumper on a car. That's not the type of damage we are dealing with here, but it is undoubtedly a more significant damage than the financial losses. It can't be recovered by the award of dollars, but you have to do something to acknowledge the seriousness of it; lost dollars can always be recovered, lost dignity and the type of trauma and life she has really lived the last three years that has consumed her.

"You heard testimony from her recently, the last three years, she has been unhealthy, she cries a lot, she has been depressed, she has been medicated. These are things that are foreign to her. She is a survivor and self-sufficient, and she hasn't been able to be self-sufficient, and what that does to her being I think you will have to use your best judgment in coming up with something that needs to acknowledge the seriousness of that impact. And I leave it obviously to you to consider that.

"The last amount of damages, the last component is separate from compensatory damages. Compensatory damages are designed to compensate the plaintiff if she has been wronged to make up for the damages inflicted upon her for the losses. Punitive damages in contrast is where the jury gets to express its opinion, its belief, it sends a message, speaking as the conscience of our community. This is the best part of our jury system. We, with all due respect to judges who are wise and everything, the jury system is what our system is built upon, and that's because the jury system is the community. It speaks for—and you are most definitely speaking for the community in this case, and believe you me, the community is watching this.

"The purpose of punitive damages is to send a clear message to the parties for starters, but to send a clear message to the defendant and to others like it, that the jury disapproves of the conduct such as that which is brought out in this case.

"How do you send such a message? Well, one thing you need to do is figure out how loudly do you need to speak to have the defendant hear you. This is a company, Yarmouth Group and Tabor Associates, look if you would at Defendant's Exhibit E and F. It's a letterhead of Yarmouth Group. This has their letterhead reflecting they have offices in New York and Atlanta and London. They have offices in Chicago, Los Angeles, San Francisco, Paris, Singapore. Mr. Hill testified that they are based in Sydney, Australia. It's right on Defendant's Exhibit D and E, I think, or maybe E and F. This is a big old company, and you need to be able to make a statement that impresses them.

"And my partner, Mr. Miller, suggested to me, and I think it's a good one, the statement needs to be heard all the way to Sydney, Australia, where they are based on the other side of the world. If you have a ma-and-pa grocery store, punitive damages for a hundred million dollars would be heard. If you award, in contrast, $500,000 or a million dollars against the Yarmouth Group, what message are you saying? Well, Yarmouth will hear that by hearing we won. A million dollars, no big deal. We won, and if you send them—if you vote in favor of Ms. Foote and find punitive damages it can't be an unclear message.

"I ended my opening statement by asking you to express in your verdict—you don't get to talk about it—you need to fill out a form and you need to be clear and forthright as to what it is you are saying, and in the punitive damages award that is what the law gives you, that voice to be clear on that. And don't allow it to be an amount where the defendants say we have won. And you know, how do you calculate that? Well, some companies just fold this into the cost of doing business. It's just another business expense. We pay lawyers, we pay expert witnesses, we pay some jury verdicts, but as long as it doesn't get too expensive it's business as usual. And if it's business as usual then the jury hasn't been heard and certainly change hasn't been made. It has to be some amount that makes business as usual bad business.

"I don't pretend to think that we can teach corporations like Yarmouth Group to be moral or to have the values that we have in this country, but we don't have to. We just need to speak their language. We need to say that this isn't good for our bottom line so don't do it anymore. We shouldn't convince them that's wrong because that won't—one, I mean if you think it will, I don't think it will. We need to speak that language and that language is the language of the bottom line.

"And I suggest then in your best judgment, in your discretion, that you award, in order to make this a signal to them, we can even make an agreement that if you award some multiple of the compensatory damages, some round multiple, I mean almost to the dollar because you don't get to actually voice an opinion, you don't get to talk to the plaintiff or to the defendants, you can give them some round multiple five times, ten times, whatever your discretion allows you to give that would be enough to make the point to them we really think that this is wrong. We really adhere to the principles that we learned in our 8th grade civics class.

"Every now and then a case like this comes along that sort of jolts us, jolts David Miller and I and our partners into why we did this in the first place. This is the type of case that we became lawyers for. And it's easy enough to get jaded and cynical. There [are] a lot of crummy cases out there. There is a lot of cases that I guess slam-dunk cases, but they might be breach of contract or argument over a dog bite, and those are important to the parties certainly, but this case is why federal courts exist, really.

"We have the enforcement of fundamental federally protected rights, and this is why we do what we do, and that's why I emphasize, really implore you to believe that this case you are sitting on is not the run-of-the-mill. It's an important case. And I think it's as plain as black and white, frankly. The principles that I suggested in the outset I think have been fulfilled by the presentation of the evidence. It's a case about equal opportunity for everybody. It's a case about the equal protection of our laws, and the protection of our most—all of our most fundamental civil rights.

"I ask you once again then in conclusion to commit to these principles, and I ask you not to compromise them. Thank you. Good luck in your deliberations."

I could almost hear the countdown of the referee start with Darold's words . . . 10, 9, 8 . . . it was a slam dunk in the strongest sense and made my eyes well up at the strength of what he had said. He had summed up my life of the last couple years and the emotion I felt at hearing it all in open court left me speechless, as if his voice had replaced mine. It had in a sense. I pulled a tissue from my jacket pocket and dabbed at the corner of my eyes. The judge had called for a recess at the conclusion of Darold's closing, so I rose and greeted him with a tight hug. "Thank you so much. What you said was incredible." My voice started to waver as I spoke and my feelings were suddenly at the back of my throat.

"You're welcome, Tseghe. I meant every word," he replied as I pulled away. I forced a smile and excused myself. I wanted to hold it in until I was in private. Once I reached the ladies' room, I went into a stall and sat down on the closed toilet lid as my body started to shake and my sobs came out in ragged gasps. I didn't want anyone to hear me and I just needed to let go of it all. As much as I had cried, so much was still bottled up. Hearing all of the hurts summarized like that had made it surface again. Maybe it was a little relief at it almost being over. I don't know.

When my sobs finally ceased, I quickly blew my nose, checked my face in the mirror, and splashed it with a little water. Almost back to normal. I had become nearly a master of the quick-cry-in-the-bathroom thing. The judge was just coming back as I took my place at the plaintiff's table. It was time for the defense's closing statement.

Still buoyed by Darold's speech, Grunschlag's closing barely affected me. It was hollow words coming from a hollow face. I saw his lips moving, but I didn't hear the sound of his voice. The world had suddenly ground to a halt around me and was now barely moving forward in time. It was one of those surreal moments when your life is happening as if you are not a participant. I could hear some of what he said about me, but it was from a far-away place. So, when his voice stopped and the judge spoke, I was startled by the sound. It was over. The jury was in recess for the weekend and we would finish up on Monday. The lawyers and the judge haggled over verdict forms and jury instructions a bit and then I was getting up to walk out. It still wasn't over. Another weekend to await my fate.

Chapter 10

Undisputed Champion

Nobody wins unless everybody wins.
—Bruce Springsteen

I spent a sleepless weekend at my apartment with friends and family calling, asking me out for dinner—anything to get my mind off of what was still to come. Mengasha spent a lot of the weekend with me, quietly watching TV beside me, as he put his active social life on hold. Everyone was anxious and worried about me, and I was very touched. I couldn't seem to sit still for long, though, as my mind raced with thoughts—What if this? What if that?

Sunday was the Super Bowl and Denver was playing for the third year in a row. They were victorious for the second and final time of the three Super Bowl visits and we were all pretty sure that this would be Elway's last game as quarterback. I watched the images flicker on the screen as Elway, Mike Shanahan, and the owner, Pat Bowlan, made their victory speeches. I wondered if the world watching could possibly have any idea of the Denver I now knew. The Denver that had let its power brokers run over me as if I were expendable. Amidst all of the kindness and support from many gracious people, I couldn't shake the hurt I felt from the handful who wanted me out. I fought against the bitterness that wasn't my nature as I heard the yells of revelers celebrating the victory of the city's beloved Broncos below me in the streets.

I lay awake in the darkness all night on Sunday and watched the sun come up on the Denver skyline through the window from the chair in my bedroom. Today was the day.

I didn't have to be in court until 10:00 because the lawyers and judge still had to settle business issues, so I went to Africa House early and sat down amongst my cherished art. In the early morning quiet, the faces on the masks and sculptures soothed me and reminded me of my purpose. I could almost sense the souls of my people, the ones who had lovingly molded these creations, gathering around me in a band of support. I wondered aloud what the day would hold for me. I knew they had no answers for me, but I also knew what those artists needed to hear.

Soon enough, I was back in the courtroom seated at the table. The room filled and it was back to business. Darold stood to give his rebuttal, and my eyes followed him as he rose. Soon, his words floated over me again, reinforcing my inner peace from days before. He didn't speak long and, as he concluded and took his seat, Judge Sparr started his instructions to the jury.

As I had maintained, the money was not part of it for me. I never wanted to settle and only asked to let my store stay open at the Tabor Center with a public apology from them. They only wanted to give me money and have me go away. So, it was with particular interest that I heard Judge Sparr mention damages during his instructions. "If you find the defendants unlawfully discriminated against the plaintiffs, but do not find that the plaintiffs suffered any actual damages, then you must award plaintiffs some nominal sum, such as one dollar, in damages." Monetary damages had become the only way the jury could strongly communicate their decision for me, if they found in my favor.

The jury began deliberations at a little before noon on Monday. My stomach did flips as I left the building with Darold and David to have lunch and begin the wait. The judge had asked us all to stay close by in case of questions or a quick verdict. Confetti covered the ground along the Broncos victory parade route from earlier in the day. I pointed it out to Darold, who didn't miss the irony. We were in court while the city celebrated. Now, we didn't really have a lot to say and our nervousness bounced off of one another like moths at a lighted window. At 4:45p.m., the jury still had not reached a verdict and we had another night ahead of us to wait—at least.

I went to Darold and David's office the next morning at 9:30. The jury was to start deliberations at 9:00 and I wanted to be close by in case anything happened. Their office was a short walk from the courthouse and seemed the logical place to wait. Four hours passed before the clerk called. The jury had reached a verdict and court started back up at 1:55p.m.

The butterflies danced in my stomach as I took my chair. I was back in that boxing ring again and could almost see someone going down. The bad part was I couldn't see yet who it was on the ground.

"Has the jury reached a verdict?" Judge Sparr asked, his voice booming across the room.

"Yes, we have," answered the foreman.

"Would you please convey the verdict to the marshals. Thank you. All right. Now hearken to the reading of the verdict. In the United States District Court for the District of Colorado in civil action 96–S-2516, *The Guides, Limited doing business as Africa House and Tseghe Foote v. Yarmouth Group Property Management, Inc. and Tabor Center Associates.* Plaintiff Tseghe Foote's discrimination claims sub 1, on Ms. Foote's discrimination claims against the defendants under 41 United States Code, 1981, we find the defendants are liable for discrimination against Ms. Foote on the basis of race under 1981. That is checked. . . . On Ms. Foote's discrimination claim against defendants under 42 United States Code, 1982, we find the defendants are liable for discrimination against Ms. Foote on the basis of race under 1982 is checked. . . . On plaintiff Africa House's discrimination claim. On Africa House's discrimination claim against the defendants under 42 United States Code, 1981, we find the defendants are liable for discrimination against Africa House on the basis of race under 1981. It's checked . . . On Africa House's discrimination claim against the defendants under 42 United States Code, 1982, we find the defendants are liable for discrimination against Africa House on the basis of race under 1982 is checked. . . . On the claims under intentional interference with prospective business advantage on paragraph 5. On Africa House's claim for intentional interference with prospective business advantage against the defendants, we find the defendants are liable for interfering with Africa House's prospective business advantage with its retail clientele. It is checked. . . .

"Damages. If you believe Ms. Foote is entitled to recover damages for—from the defendants, in what amount of damages do you award on Ms. Foote's claims for relief? You said the compensatory damage blank the figure $200,000 appears. Under the punitive damage claims the figure $1,500,000 appears. Subsection 7, if you believe Africa House is entitled to recover compensatory damages from the defendants, then what amount of compensatory damages do you award to Africa House on all claims for relief? The figure $150,000 appears. Under 8, if you believe that Africa House is to recover punitive damages from the defendant, then what amount of punitive damages do you award to Africa House on its claims under 42 United States Code, 1981, and 42 United States Code, 1982? The figure one million appears."

The world paused on its axis as the words sank in. I had really and truly won. The jury had believed in me and I had justice at long last. I stole a quick glance at Grunschlag and his clients and their faces showed nothing but shock and disbelief. How could it be that both sides would have the same reaction? I couldn't trust my ears though. As soon as the judge dismissed the jurors for the last time and adjourned court, I turned to Darold. "What did he just say? Is it really true?"

He swept me up in a hug and yelled, "Yes! It's true! You won! You won!"

Tears streamed down my face in joy for the first time in years. Gloria and Mengasha rushed up to me and hugged me too. We were all crying and hugging and kissing each other as the unbelievable feeling of relief swept us up. It was over and we had won. As the moment wound down a bit, Darold grabbed my arm, "Tseghe? Did you hear the damages they gave you?"

I had barely been able to hear anything after those initial phrases that pronounced the judgment in my favor. "No. What did they say?"

"Tseghe, the jury awarded you $2.85 million."

My ears rang at his words. "What?! Are you kidding me?" I couldn't believe it and don't think it really sank in fully until I saw the front page of *The*

Rocky Mountain News the next day. I had made headlines just a day after the Broncos had been front page news. *Shop Owner Wins $2.85 Million in Discrimination Suit.*

When I reached Africa House the next day, word of my victory had spread, and well-wishers crowded the store to congratulate me. Champagne flowed and flashbulbs of reporters popped at various photo opportunities. Even people who had turned their backs on me along the duration came to apologize and congratulate me on my tenacity. The celebration in my heart was a sweeter victory than any dollar amount could have created. I stood in the middle of the ring with my boxing gloves off, basking in my victory. I raised my fist to the ceiling as the crowd swelled around me, and shouted, "Yes!"

Chapter 11

Defending the Title

Justice is such a fine thing that we cannot pay too dearly for it.

—Alain Rene' Lesage

I had little time to savor the victory before the post-trial motions began. It started in February when the judge entered the judgment, ordering both the Tabor Center and Yarmouth to pay by issuing a $4 million bond for each company. Their response was to hire additional lawyers to help fight the appeal. Lawyers educated at prestigious learning institutions like Princeton and Columbia. By the time all was said and done, there were seven lawyers working for the defense. It made me laugh to think that it was Darold, David, and me against this large group of Ivy Leaguers.

A deposition was called to have the Tabor Center and Yarmouth Associates present their financials and their plan for paying the judgment. The lawyers for the defense never showed. I was in shock. I couldn't believe that they just hadn't shown up. Darold then sent a letter to the magistrate judge asking for action against the defense.

In response to the letter, the judge called a hearing. As we arrived in court, I had a strong sense of déjà vu. It had only been a couple of short months since the courtroom had been my home. I shuddered as I put my purse on the conveyor and walked through the security check. Magistrate Judge Bruce Pringle was presiding and immediately declared the Yarmouth Group in contempt of court, since they still had not issued the bond. The Tabor Center had issued the bond at the time of the order. Now, the Yarmouth Group would be fined $2,500 a day until they complied with the order, plus would be required to pay my lawyer's legal fees. Then court was adjourned. It never even occurred to me that they would try to avoid paying me once the jury had reached a verdict. I expected an appeal, but never outright avoidance. It was unbelievable. It only got worse.

The answer to the contempt charge came within a couple of days. It was an affidavit that claimed the Yarmouth Group was bankrupt and no longer existed. Judge Pringle forwarded it all back to Judge Sparr to handle. Judge Sparr was livid. He called a hearing that all of the lawyers involved were ordered to attend. They flew in from both coasts this time—Atlanta and San Francisco—to give their explanation of this latest turn of events. Judge Sparr was not the type to take a jury verdict lightly and did not appreciate defendants who did.

It was June when the hearing was called and it was back to the courtroom for us. *The Denver Post* covered the event and ran a story on June 16, 1999, on the front page of the business section with the headline, "Winning lawsuit doesn't end battle." Darold was quoted saying, "All of this activity is legal maneuvering to avoid accountability, no question about it." The defense had no comment.

When the defense lawyers were called upon to explain this affidavit, that was, in Judge Sparr's estimation, in violation of a clear verdict, they immediately backpedaled and apologized. I sat in my seat and watched these supposedly prestigious lawyers squirm. I guess a judge can have that effect on even the most seasoned attorney. "Your Honor," they said. "We owe the court an apology. Yarmouth Group merged last December with a new owner. We assumed that meant we were considered bankrupt, but actually it was simply a merger. We apologize for our confusion. The good news is that we are now an even bigger company, so Ms. Foote doesn't have to worry about getting her money."

I was astounded. Did they truly think that we would all buy that they didn't know the difference between a merger and bankruptcy? It was amazing the lengths they would go to play games with me, the jury, the court, and the public at large. It seemed so blatant to me that they had tried to decrease their liability by using this merger as an excuse. They showed it had happened two months before the trial, but never mentioned it in court. In fact, Office Equity Property, the merged companies' new name, was never anywhere in a public record. I had only heard the new name through the grapevine and had assumed it was an entirely new owner. I thought it would mean a clean slate, but it was only the Yarmouth Group in disguise. It seemed the cover-up would go on forever. The verdict had taught them nothing.

Judge Sparr excused them from the contempt charges, convinced that they would at last pay up. I had my doubts since they had maintained the status quo—still with the same managers and owners—just a slight name change with a name they weren't actually using anywhere. Every day I went to my store, I had the possibility of running into Dan Hill or any of them. I didn't trust them at all. But, the hearing ended and we went on our way for the time being.

Another month or so went by and we received—not a check—but a post-trial motion filed by the defense, calling for a judgment to reduce the amount of the settlement or give a new trial since they claimed we hadn't presented enough evidence at this one. Judge Sparr scheduled a hearing for August 2, 1999.

By now, I had lost the original feelings of anxiety brought on by this courtroom. This courtroom scene had become old hat. I even recognized the security guard at the front as I walked in.

The hearing started with motions by the defense to get a new trial. Darold argued our side, they argued theirs, and the judge denied their motion. I was relieved, but felt almost robotic about the whole thing. It had a mechanical feel and I was devoid of any emotion. I think I was just so tired and cried out by this point that I couldn't feel anything. At times, it was like they were talking about someone else.

The next motion involved the verdict. The defense argued that I had no legal standing as an individual and that the damages awarded to me personally should be withdrawn. We argued that Africa House is me—that I am interchangeable with it. But, to no avail. We held our breath as Judge Sparr agreed and took away over half of my award—$1,700,000. His decision was a complete contradiction to the judgment he had entered only a couple of months before—supporting that I did have legal standing as an individual. Now, I didn't count anymore. I was simply the corporation called The Guides. That was it. Court adjourned. I stared at the judge's back as he returned to his chambers. He had turned his back on me in more ways than one.

So, the next few months consisted of me maintaining what was left of my store since I didn't have to be out until the case was finalized. I moved through the months in a trance. My customer base had dwindled. The publicity had not been favorable since most of the media had portrayed me as an opportunist—leaving out crucial details in their reports. The public had believed what they read and, for the most part, had turned away.

I appealed the judge's decision in an effort to regain the jury's judgment and re-coup my legal fees. The Tabor Center appealed the jury's judgment for the corporate damages I was awarded, on the same basis they had used for the motion against me as an individual. It seemed it would never end. I was absolutely appalled that this could continue to drag on for so long after I thought I had won. The jury had ruled in my favor, I had won the case, yet I was still having to fight the system. Finally, both appeals were set to be heard by the Court of Appeals the following summer in 2000.

While I went through the motions of living and awaited this one last effort, I tried to find some positive aspects to the whole situation. I focused on the few friends and family who had been so supportive. Then, in the middle of the back-and-forth drama with the courts, I received notice in the mail that I was to be honored by the Colorado Civil Rights Division, et. al., with a Community Builder Award. The award was given to people in the community who "build community in the face of bigotry and hate." I almost laughed out loud as I read the letter. This was the very same group of people who had dismissed my case and left me to fend for myself years before—now they were honoring me. What a turn of events! After much soul searching, I decided to take the high road and accept the award with appreciation.

Fast forward to March 2000. I was still waiting for the appeal when the last straw came by mail. It was a letter from the Tabor Center that effectively evicted me from the premises, despite all that had happened. It explained that "renovation plans will require the complete closure of most of the first and second floors of the Tabor Center once under full construction. Accordingly, we are beginning work with the affected tenants to make arrangements for their temporary or permanent relocation or the termination of their lease . . . the space available for temporary or permanent relocation is extremely limited and we are obligated to accommodate certain tenants pursuant to the terms of their lease." Which meant no Africa House. They couldn't tell me when exactly—but no matter what, it looked like I would no longer exist by the end of the year 2000.

I heard on the news that the ESPN Sports Bar would be moving in once the renovations were complete and I couldn't help but wonder how they would feel if they knew the history of their new landlords to be.

The appeal was heard. . . . .

Chapter 12

The Following Describes What Happened from 2000 to 2007…

FOR THE CASE:

Interviewer: What was the result of the Appeal?

T.F: We heard all the jokes about lawyers, but when it happens to you, it's not a joke anymore. It's a nightmare. According to Judges Brisoe, McWilliams and Jenkins:

> "The decision of the district court dismissing Foote for lack of standing is AFFIRMED. We VACATE the judgment and direct the district court to dismiss Africa House's claim of intentional interference with prospective business advantages. We REVERSE the district court's denial of the defendants' request for a remittitur and REMAND with directions that the district court enter a remittitur order reducing the compensatory damages awarded to

Africa House to $75,316.95 or, in the alternative, to grant a new trial. We AFFIRM the district court's denial of the defendants' motion for a new trial for alleged evidentiary errors. We REVERSE the district court's denial of the defendants' motion for judgment as a matter of law as to the punitive damages awarded to Africa House and VACATE the award of punitive damages. We REVERSE the district court's order granting prejudgment interest at the state rate from the date the claim accrued, and REMAND for a determination of the rate of prejudgment interest and for a determination of the date or dates of accrual. We AFFIRM the district court's award of attorney fees."
(see Addendum)

According to Judge Jenkins, Senior District Judge, concurring and dissenting:

"The majority relies on Gersman v. Group Health Association. Inc., 931 F.2d 1565 (D.C. Cir. 1991), vacated on other grounds, 502 U.S. 1068 (1992), to hold that 'Africa House has standing to assert discrimination claims under § 1981 and § 1982 where such discrimination is based on the race of one of its employees.'

"I agree with the reasoning in Gersman, and I agree that the jury correctly found that Africa House suffered an injury resulting from unlawful discrimination. However, the jury also found that the defendants had discriminated against Ms. Foote because of her race and that Ms. Foote suffered a compensable injury distinct from that suffered by Africa House. Ms. Foote, as is required by our prior cases, is a member of the protected class under sections 1981 and 1982 and was the direct target of the defendants' racial discrimination whether she was acting in her individual capacity in seeking to enter into the prospective lease contract, or was acting as agent for her corporation. She is entitled to redress for her own injuries that also fall clearly within the zone of interests protected by sections 1981 and 1982. The defendants caused injury both to Africa House and Ms. Foote by refusing to deal with Ms. Foote—a refusal the jury found to be racially motivated. Affirming the defendants' liability to the corporate plaintiff, Africa House, acknowledges that the corporation suffered an injury resulting from unlawful discrimination—racial discrimination for which Ms. Foote served as the very human direct target."

His conclusion was:

"The jury found in Ms. Foote's favor, awarding her $200,000 in damages . . . I would therefore hold that both Africa House and Ms. Foote have standing to assert the section 1981 and 1982 causes of action against the defendants, and that the district court's ruling as to Ms. Foote should be reversed and judgment in favor of Ms. Foote should be reinstated as to compensatory damages."
(see Addendum)

Interviewer: How did you find out?

T.F.: I found out from a phone call from Darold Killmer who said, "We won our case, but it's not $4 million anymore, it's $75,000 plus interest. And we got $200,000 for legal fees."

Interviewer: If the judgment was for $2.85 million, where did $4 million come from?

T.F: According to the law, the defendant was supposed to pay interest from the day I filed the temporary injunction in October 1996 until the final decision of the 10th Circuit U.S. Court of Appeals in July 2002. And for legal fees and expenses.
(see Addendum)

Interviewer: Was the Appeal decided correctly?

T.F.: In my opinion, no, because basically the jury saw my case and, in the end, they made the right decision [to award me $2.85 million]. However, the Court decided the testimony of the expert witness, Dr. Kaempfer, for loss of profit was only $75,000.

Dr. Kaempfer didn't care about the integrity of my case. He came to testify without knowing or having any knowledge of my case. He never met me. He never saw my store. He never talked to any of my customer "witnesses," because my customers couldn't find me since my store was closed for 10 days in the process of moving from the west side of the mall to the east side of the mall—completely different malls. He never saw my legal paperwork, such as the temporary injunction. He didn't know I had to move out after the case ended. He didn't know that my business circumstances were pending on the summary judgment. The only information he had was that Killmer told him we have a lady that moved her business from one location to another location due to race bias. They only talked for 45 minutes. Dr. Kaempfer also didn't know that I had to spend a lot of money to re-locate my store, and $6,000 for legal fees for David Fine to file temporary injunction and to stop the eviction, and pay for my severe illnesses due to tremendous stress. Whatever information he had was in 1997, and the trial did not happen until 1999. By then it was too late to submit the right information into the trial. So the first time I actually saw him was on the witness stand when he was trying to calculate the damages of the business. He testified to one amount, but the judge had to excuse the jury and find out what the correct amount was from Kaempfer. By then he had admitted he made a mistake. My lawyers did not properly prepare him for the trial. Dr. Kaempfer admitted all the above problems in his deposition during the legal malpractice case against my lawyers.

Interviewer: Do you feel confident in our justice system now?

T.F.: No. I thought the justice system would work for me where even I could challenge one of the biggest corporations and high-powered lawyers. It says a lot about this country that the power of this country is in the hands of the wonderful people like my jurors. The "factfinders" were supposed to be the jury, however, their decision was replaced by the three judges. Therefore, I didn't get the judgment by my "peers," but by three judges.

Interviewer: Why was there so much confusion between the Jury decisions and the Appeal decisions?

T.F.: Read the Allegations document for the malpractice case in the Addendum.

FOR THE SETTLEMENT:

Interviewer: What happened after the Court of Appeals decision?

T.F.: For almost close to a year, Killmer ignored me. However, we settled the case with a non-disclosed amount.
(see Addendum)

FOR NEGLIGENCE (legal malpractice):

Interviewer: How did you discover that there was legal malpractice, and what did you do about it?

T.F.: During the year I was waiting for Killmer to consult with me, I contacted a legal malpractice lawyer because I wanted to get opinions about why I lost the jury verdict. The legal malpractice lawyer, Charles Welton, after reading the U.S Court of Appeals decision, decided to hire expert witnesses [Patrick LeHouillier] to see if there was legal malpractice. And then the expert witness confirmed it was legal malpractice. I had pain and suffering documented by Dr. Egan [who was not my official doctor]. Therefore I had grounds to sue my former lawyers for not calling my official doctor [during the Federal case] to testify to my pain and suffering. (see Addendum)

Interviewer: So did Dr. Egan testify for the malpractice case?

T.F.: Yes. However, the sitting judge's [Judge Catherine Lemon] choice was not to allow the jury to decide on Dr. Egan's expert testimony concerning my past and future pain and suffering. This was her diagnosis:

> "Patient has Grave's disease that has been exacerbated by a very difficult lawsuit that has resulted in the closing of her business, premature menopause, osteoporosis and HTN, and extreme anxiety with insomnia. Patient has been unable to work since July 2001 & case finally comes to court [trial] in June 2005. Disability is of indefinite duration."

Thanks to Dr. Egan. She saved my life!

In my opinion, the judges, including Judge Lemon, are still reading the "Old School Book" where Blacks aren't supposed to get paid for their pain and suffering. (see Addendum)

Interviewer: What was the outcome of the legal malpractice case?

T.F.: The jury decided in my favor for "damages or losses" [$176,600] and for "breach of fiduciary duty" [$13,924] when the jury found them guilty of negligence on five counts. However, I didn't receive any pain and suffering compensation thanks to Judge Lemon. A "domino effect" of errors occurred starting with the expert witnesses to Mr. Welton's instructions to the jury.

I have been emotionally tortured and financially ruined by David Miller, Darold Killmer, and Charles Welton.
(see Addendum)

Interviewer: Sounds like you lost another jury verdict?

T.F.: In principle I won. The jury believed me and spoke on my behalf. I stood up to find out the truth, but it was stolen by the judges and the lawyers all over again.

Interviewer: So you must be very disappointed by the outcome?

T.F.: Yes. And so I hired a new lawyer and appealed to find out what happened. The new lawyer suggested I speak to a malpractice specialist immediately about suing Charles Welton. But I didn't do it because Welton spent all my money [$60,000] plus $18,000 to appeal the decision. There wasn't any money left to hire a new lawyer. I didn't want to file another malpractice suit. Besides, by this time I had totally lost faith in the system working for me like it's supposed to work. It took 11 years from 1996 to 2007 to fight the injustice.

Interviewer: Do you think the two sitting juries, one Federal (for discrimination) and one State (for legal malpractice), would be satisfied with the Judges' reversed decisions?

T.F: No. They would say, in my opinion, the government disappointed her before, and now the government disappointed us.

In the end, I didn't go to court to find out what my business would sell for. My business wasn't for sale. My business was my life. All those years I fought to make the lawyers rich. Even the "negligence" lawyers walked away with $250,000, and the problem is still there. To my lawyers, I was one of many clients. They didn't care if I had a business or not! They still have a functioning business. My case was, and is, full of corruption!

This fight should not have been my fight. It should have been the government's fight, but my government let me down. The judges let the jury down when they tried to do the right thing to send a message that diversity is good for our community, and freedom is good for everybody.

This book is to honor all the people of this country. We give strength to each other to make this country a better country.

Epilogue

The Prizefighter

Tout comprendre c'est tout pardonner. To understand is to forgive all.

—Mme de Stael

When I arrived in America, I was an innocent child with an open heart. I knew only complete acceptance since racial divisions did not exist in Ethiopia, since we were never colonized. I had only seen whites and blacks working together for a common goal, as the kindness of American Peace Corps workers was a prevalent influence in my young life. I saw America as a land of further opportunity and kindness. A place where my dreams would come true.

When I arrived in America, I was enchanted with the new way of life. It seemed that anything was possible if I worked hard enough. I was in awe of the immense amount of opportunity that was mine for the taking. My love affair with America stayed intact as I established my business and my life in this new land. It wasn't until this unfortunate chain of events that the honeymoon abruptly ended.

It was truly frightening to me to be suddenly be surrounded by people with such closed minds and hearts. The divisions leapt out at me and I could see clearly for the first time how these people were deliberately elevating themselves above me. It seemed I had moved into a war zone of sorts. I had left my own country with its physical war, and found myself in the middle of a war that was so subtle that it moved in the shadows and you couldn't anticipate who the enemy was or what the next move would be. I was introduced to a societal war where judging your fellow man was common practice. The same type of judgment that had caused an era's worth of great Hollywood legends to be destroyed. No one wanted to get involved, even when they knew something was wrong and criminal. Self-preservation at its finest. It was all unfathomable to someone like me who had never experienced this subtle form of manipulation and exclusion.

When I struck out on my own and started my business, I felt that the American dream was mine at last. I had worked hard, done the right things, and I was accepted in the business community and embraced by many affluent people—both white and black. Ten years of running a successful business, despite a bad economy and a number of forced relocations, and I thought I was paving the way for my eventual retirement. Then, the bottom dropped out right when I thought I had it made.

Imagine how it felt to be told that "you aren't glamorous enough" when Shaquille O'Neill or Kevin Johnson has just left your store with an armload of merchandise. When nearly every celebrity who came to Denver and stayed in the Westin Hotel at the Tabor Center had browsed in your store and bought something. It was those words that gave me the will to fight. I knew in my heart that what they were doing was wrong and was based on something uglier and more vile than my childlike innocence could imagine. My store was the soul of who I was and they were attacking it, calling it expendable and taking it away from me in the process. Suddenly, I felt true fear. My store and my innocence were snatched away from me with that one short phase—"you aren't glamorous enough . . . it's the whole thing." I wasn't being treated equally as a human being any more—I was now being treated as an outsider, a black, a woman, an immigrant.

The issue goes much further than being gay or a woman or a member of a certain racial group. It is everyone's problem—it is our problem as a society and a nation. It isn't about righting the wrongs of the past and throwing stones, it is about fighting against the divisions put in place by ignorance and fear. Fear and ignorance cause discrimination and minds and hearts that are closed are very difficult to open. Ultimately, negative thinking could destroy our country. So, we have to do something—anything. The only solution is bonding together for a common goal: building understanding.

Teach the Children. The best place to start is with children. By teaching them to accept and appreciate diversity, they will maintain their innocence and will stay open to other cultures, races, and societies. Their lives will be full. Full of the excitement of trying a new food for the first time, hearing a new song, or learning a new ritual. Teach them not to fear differences, and when they are grown, they will not have to feel fear like I have felt. Teach them to celebrate diversity and our country will become a more accepting place in a few short years. If they frown on ignorance and are joyful at enlightenment, society will be a better place for us all.

Call People on It. Refuse to accept unfair treatment. We all have to take a stand when faced with adversity and say, "NOT ACCEPTABLE." It would have been so much easier for me to just close my business and find a job somewhere, but my heart wouldn't let me. I wanted to right the wrong and make the Tabor Center and Yarmouth Group apologize. I simply wanted to stay in business and they took that option away from me. In the three years they took to attempt to destroy my business, they could have spent time learning about me, my store, my clientele, and my culture. They could have admitted they made a mistake, and everything would have been okay. One day I was a business owner and the next I was a crusader. Now, as a result, I have become a community leader. All I wanted to do was open their minds to me and give me a chance without judgment.

So, stand up for yourself. It is the only way to make a difference and no one can stand up for you but you.

Know Your Options. There are many resources available to you, but don't trust just one. The Colorado Civil Rights Commission failed me when I went to them first. But, instead of giving up, I decided to continue fighting. Don't let one person or group discourage you when your heart is telling you that you have been wronged. Be strong and determined and "Endeavor to Persevere." Exhaust all avenues and elicit the support of your friends and family. If they won't support you, find people who will. Question everything and everyone and educate yourself. You will need all of the resources and information you can get to fight.

Know Your Corporations. People have more ability than ever before to make educated consumer decisions. Take advantage of the wealth of information available to you in the media and on the Internet. Don't support companies who discriminate, and you will send an important message. Corporations need your support to exist, and, if you hold them accountable for their actions, you are bound to see results. In addition, insurance doesn't cover discrimination suits against corporations, so if you choose to sue, you will send a message directly to their pocketbooks. Juries are determined to get to the truth and will punish perpetrators of discrimination of any kind. I am living proof of that.

We have a new generation of people and consumers who, by working together, can truly make a difference. Being brave enough to create diversity in companies' cultures and thinking in terms of the bigger picture is the way of this new generation of thinkers. More disabled, women, minorities, and gays are in leadership roles today than ever before. The majority is becoming more diverse, and leaders and politicians should represent that effectively. We shouldn't stand for it to be any other way. Lines that have divided us for hundreds of years, while still there in some places, have virtually disappeared in online communities on the Internet. We shouldn't tolerate anything else.

I felt compelled to share my story to inspire others to fight for their rights and affect social change. Racism and discrimination hurts everyone, not just individuals. As history has shown, it can tear apart entire communities and nations. If you fall victim to it, you must stick with your truth and fight it with everything you have. No matter how painful the fight was for me, I wouldn't have had it any other way. I couldn't let a company just come in and shatter my dreams with no repercussions. There is still a lot of work to be done, but if we work together we can chip away at it, bit by bit. I can now give boxing lessons to anyone needing guidance in winning the fight.

There may be times when we are powerless to prevent injustice, but there must never be a time when we fail to protest.

—Elie Wiesel

Sources

Ethiopian history and geography adapted from Microsoft *Encarta* Encyclopedia 2000. 1993–1999 Microsoft Corporation.

Excerpts taken from transcripts from *The Guides, Ltd. D/b/a The Africa House vs. The Yarmouth Group Property Management. Inc., and Tabor Center Associates,* commencing January 25, 1999.

Headlines from *Denver Post*, Friday, October 26, 1984, section B, and *Denver Post*, June 16, 1999, Business section B

Headline from *Rocky Mountain News*, February 3, 1999, section A, page 5.

Addendum

MILLER, LANE, KILLMER & GREISEN, LLP
730 17TH ST. • SUITE 600 • DENVER, COLORADO 80202
ATTORNEYS AT LAW

DAVID H. MILLER
DAVID A. LANE
DAROLD W. KILLMER
PAULA GREISEN

303.534.6400
FAX: 303.534.0156
E-MAIL: mklaw@usa.net

October 20, 1998

Tseghe Foote
The Africa House
The Shops at Tabor Center
1201 16th Street, Suite 202
Denver, Colorado 80202

Re: *The Africa House vs. The Yarmouth Group Property Management, Inc.*
U.S. District Court Case No. 96-S-2516

Dear Tseghe:

This letter confirms the advice that our law firm has given you with regard to the settlement negotiations in this case. During the settlement talks last week, you informed me that you did not want to settle this case for money, but rather required that the case proceed to trial. While we are perfectly willing to bring this case to trial, we believe that to refuse to consider settlement on any monetary terms is a mistake.

The defendants had offered $100,000 to settle this case, and all indications were that they would go significantly higher. Indeed, Magistrate Judge Pringle was estimating that he may get them to settle somewhere between $200,000 and $300,000. That is a significant amount of money, and worthy of your serious consideration. We personally believe that if a settlement could be achieved in the neighborhood of $300,000, it should be taken. As noted above, however, the choice is yours, and if you advise us to go to trial, we will do so zealously.

As you know, we have discussed at length the many risks involved in this litigation. There is a pending Motion for Summary Judgment which seeks to throw the whole case out. While we do not believe this motion should prevail, it is entirely possible that Judge Sparr could grant it, in which case the case could be over, subject to our right to appeal. Appeals, by the way, are very difficult and time consuming.

In addition, while we believe the case has merit, a jury might disagree, and they could render a verdict for the defendants.

Tseghe Foote
October 20, 1998
Page 2

Finally, as you have found out several times already, delays can be frustrating and expensive. Even if we go to trial in January 1999, and even if we win, the defendants could appeal, so we are still looking at months or years before the judicial system renders a final decision. This is another advantage of settlement -- closure on the issues involved in the litigation, sooner rather than later.

Tseghe, we simply wanted to put some of these things in writing to ensure that our advice to you and explanation of your options is clear. As stated earlier, if you choose to go to trial, we will aggressively represent you in court and before the jury. We believe in you and your case.

Sincerely,

MILLER, LANE, KILLMER & GREISEN, LLP

Darold W. Killmer

David H. Miller

DWK/cb

FILE COPY
FILED
UNITED STATES DISTRICT COURT
DENVER, COLORADO
FEB - 5 1999
JAMES R. MANSPEAKER
CLERK
BY

IN THE UNITED STATES DISTRICT COURT
FOR THE DISTRICT OF COLORADO

Civil Action No. 96-S-2516

THE GUIDES, LTD., d/b/a THE AFRICA HOUSE, a Colorado corporation, and TSEGHE FOOTE, individually,

RECEIVED
FEB 08 1999

Plaintiffs,

vs.

THE YARMOUTH GROUP PROPERTY MANAGEMENT, INC., a Delaware corporation, and TABOR CENTER ASSOCIATES, L.P.,

Defendants.

JUDGMENT

This matter came on regularly for trial on the 25th day of January, 1999, before the Court, the Honorable Daniel B. Sparr, Judge presiding, and a jury of twelve persons duly sworn to try the issues herein, and on February 2, 1999, the jury returned their verdicts as follows:

1. On Plaintiff Tseghe Foote's discrimination claim against Defendants under 42 U.S.C. § 1981, the jury found that Defendants were liable for discrimination against Ms. Foote on the basis of race under § 1981.

2. On Plaintiff Tseghe Foote's discrimination claim against Defendants under 42 U.S.C. § 1982, the jury found that Defendants were liable for discrimination against Ms. Foote on the basis of race under § 1982.

3. On Africa House's discrimination claim against Defendants under 42 U.S.C. § 1981, the jury found that Defendants were liable for discrimination against Africa House on the basis of race under § 1981.

Page 2
Judgment
96-S-2516

4. On Africa House's discrimination claim against Defendants under 42 U.S.C. § 1982, the jury found that Defendants were liable for discrimination against Africa House on the basis of race under § 1982.

5. On Africa House's claim of intentional interference with prospective business advantage against the Defendants, the jury found that Defendants were liable for interfering with Africa House's prospective business advantage with its retail clientele.

6. The jury found that Plaintiff Tseghe Foote is entitled to recover damages from Defendants on her two claims for relief in the amount of $200,000.00 in compensatory damages and $1,500,000.00 in punitive damages.

7. The jury found that Plaintiff Africa House is entitled to recover compensatory damages from the Defendants on all its claims for relief in the amount of $150,000.00.

8. The jury found that Plaintiff Africa House is entitled to recover punitive damages from Defendants on its claims under 42 U.S.C. § 1981 and 42 U.S.C. § 1982 in the amount of $1,000,000.00.

9. Defendants, The Yarmouth Group Property Management, Inc. and Tabor Center Associates, L.P., stipulated on the record in open court that any judgment entered would be against both defendants jointly and severally.

It is ORDERED that judgment is entered in favor of the Plaintiffs and against the Defendants. It is

FURTHER ORDERED that judgment is entered in favor of the Plaintiff Tseghe Foot and against the Defendants, jointly and severally, in the amount of $200,000.00 in compensatory damages and $1,500,000.00 in punitive damages. It is

FURTHER ORDERED that judgment is entered in favor of the Plaintiff Africa House and against the Defendants, jointly and severally, in the amount of $150,000.00 in compensatory damages and $1,000,000.00 in punitive damages. It is

Page 3
Judgment
96-S-2516

FURTHER ORDERED that post-judgment interest shall accrue at the legal rate of 4.584% per annum from the date of entry of this judgment. It is

FURTHER ORDERED that the Plaintiffs shall have their costs upon the filing of a Bill of Costs with the Clerk of the Court within 10 days of entry of this judgment.

DATED at Denver, Colorado, this 5th day of February, 1999.

APPROVED:

DANIEL B. SPARR, JUDGE
U.S. DISTRICT COURT

FOR THE COURT:

JAMES R. MANSPEAKER, CLERK

By Yvonne M Kellogg
~~Stephen P. Ehrlich~~
~~Chief~~ Deputy

ENTERED
ON THE DOCKET

FEB - 5 1999

JAMES R. MANSPEAKER
CLERK
BY________

PUBLISH

UNITED STATES COURT OF APPEALS

TENTH CIRCUIT

FILED
United States Court of Appeals
Tenth Circuit

JUL 2 2002

PATRICK FISHER
Clerk

THE GUIDES, LTD., a Colorado limited liability company, doing business as The Africa House; and TSEGHE FOOTE, individually, Plaintiffs/Appellants/Cross-Appellees,	
v.	No. 99-1388
THE YARMOUTH GROUP PROPERTY MANAGEMENT, INC.[*]; TABOR CENTER ASSOCIATES, L.P., Defendants/Appellees/Cross-Appellants.	No. 99-1389 No. 99-1392 No. 99-1455 No. 99-1459 No. 99-1464

APPEAL FROM THE UNITED STATES DISTRICT COURT

FOR THE DISTRICT OF COLORADO

(D.C. NO. 96-S-2516)

Darold W. Killmer (David H. Miller and Mari Newman with him on the brief), Miller, Lane, Killmer & Greisen, LLP, Denver, Colorado, for the Plaintiffs/Appellants/Cross-Appellees.

Robert Lawrence Ashe, Jr., Paul, Hastings, Janofsky & Walker, LLP, Atlanta, Georgia, (Kelly J. Koelker and Maureen E. O'Neill, Paul, Hastings, Janofsky & Walker, LLP, Atlanta, Georgia; Dov M. Grunschlag, Steinhart & Falconer, LLP, San Francisco, California; and James L. Aab, Aab & Botts, LLC, Denver, Colorado, with him on the brief for Tabor Center Associates, L.P.; David H. Stacy, Elzi Pringle & Gurr, Denver, Colorado, for The Yarmouth Group Property Management, Inc., joins in the brief for Tabor Center Associates, L.P.), for the Defendants/Appellees/Cross-Appellants.

Before **BRISCOE** and **MCWILLIAMS**, Circuit Judges; and **JENKINS**, Senior District Judge.[(2)]

BRISCOE, Circuit Judge.

Plaintiffs Tseghe Foote and The Guides, Ltd., d/b/a The Africa House (hereinafter Africa House) brought a civil rights action against defendants The Yarmouth Group Property Management, Inc., and Tabor Center Associates, L.P., alleging the defendants had violated 42 U.S.C. § 1981, and had intentionally interfered with Africa House's prospective business advantages in conjunction with the defendants' eviction and failure to lease retail space for Africa House. A jury found in favor of Foote and Africa House on all counts, and awarded each plaintiff compensatory and punitive damages. Following post-trial motions, the district court dismissed Foote as an individual plaintiff for lack of standing and vacated the jury's award to her. The district court also granted Africa House's request for attorney fees, although it reduced the requested rates, and further granted prejudgment interest to Africa House.

The defendants appeal the district court's denial of their motion for judgment as a matter of law and motion for new trial or remittitur, as well as the district court's award of prejudgment interest. The plaintiffs cross-appeal the dismissal of Foote as an individual plaintiff and the reduction in attorney fees. Our jurisdiction is pursuant to 28 U.S.C. § 1291. We affirm in part, reverse in part, and remand.

I.

The Guides, Ltd., is a subchapter S corporation organized under Colorado law and doing business as The Africa House, a retail store specializing in African art and artifacts. Tseghe Foote, an immigrant from Ethiopia, is its sole shareholder and president. In 1993, Foote entered into two separate short-term lease agreements with the prior owners of the Tabor Center, a downtown mall in Denver, Colorado, for Africa House to occupy space 322 at the Center. The first short-term agreement ran from February through August of 1993, and the second ran month-to-month beginning in September 1993. Under the terms of the leases, the rent consisted of a base amount of approximately $23 per square foot, and 15% of sales above a predetermined level. The lease did not require Africa House to make any payments for mall operating costs or to incur any improvement or build-out expenses. In exchange for these favorable terms, the lease provided that the owners could terminate the tenancy or relocate the business with fifteen days' notice if they required space 322 for any reason. The possibility of relocation was dependant upon available space and the owners' judgment concerning merchandising mix and balance.

In October 1994, defendant Tabor Center Associates acquired the Tabor Center and became the plaintiffs' landlord. In February 1995, defendant Yarmouth assumed management responsibilities for the Center. In an effort to improve the profitability of the Center, Yarmouth implemented new leasing procedures that included negotiating long-term leases with future tenants. Yarmouth also approached existing tenants to negotiate new long-term and short-term tenancies. However, Yarmouth did not approach Foote, and in fact had no contact with her until September 1996 when Foote approached Yarmouth to discuss the possibility of renewing or entering into a new lease.

From this initial meeting until late October 1996, Foote had several meetings with representatives of Yarmouth concerning the possibility of leasing space at the Tabor Center. However, Yarmouth would not clarify its intentions or engage in serious negotiations. Foote and Yarmouth discussed a possible space for relocation of the business, but Yarmouth would not assure Foote that the space would be available, even though it was undisputed there were many empty spaces available at the Tabor Center. During these attempted negotiations, a representative from Yarmouth made misrepresentations to Foote concerning the lease at space 322 and commented that her store: (1) did not "mix well" with other tenants; (2) was not glamourous enough; (3) "had to go"; (4) did not "fit the image of Tabor Center"; (5) should change its name; (6) devalued the Tabor Center; and (7) was unsophisticated. Yarmouth also drew up blueprints which did not include Foote's store.

On September 13, 1996, General Nutrition Centers (GNC), a national vitamin and health chain, entered into a ten-year lease with Yarmouth for space 322 at an annual rent double that charged for Africa House. Foote was not informed of this lease while she negotiated with Yarmouth. On September 24, 1996, Foote arrived at her store to find a man making detailed measurements. When she called management to find out the purpose of the measurements, she was informed that it was an attempt to lower the insurance rates for the Center. It was only later that Foote learned that space 322 had been leased to GNC, and the measurements were made in connection with that lease.

On September 26, Yarmouth informed Foote that Africa House would not be offered a long-term lease because its gross sales did not meet or exceed $800,000. Yarmouth was also reluctant to offer Africa House a different space or a short-term lease. On October 14, 1996, the defendants served Foote with notice terminating her lease for space 322. The termination notice did not contain any offer of relocation or a short-term lease, even though other tenants who had been terminated by Yarmouth were offered such options. Foote hired an attorney to negotiate with Yarmouth. Yarmouth eventually offered Africa House a four-month lease for space 202 in the Center, but Foote rejected the lease due to its short duration.

On October 29, 1996, Foote filed the complaint in this action against Yarmouth and Tabor Center Associates, along with an application for a temporary restraining order. Before a hearing on the order, the parties stipulated to relocate the business to space 202 until the legal issues were resolved. In the complaint, Foote brought claims on her own behalf and on behalf of Africa House, alleging that the defendants had (1) unlawfully interfered with the right to make and enforce a contract, in violation of 42 U.S.C. § 1981; and (2) unlawfully interfered with the right to lease real property, in violation of 42 U.S.C. § 1982. Africa House also brought a claim alleging that the defendants had intentionally interfered with its prospective business advantages.

A jury found in favor of both Foote and Africa House on all claims. The jury awarded $200,000 in compensatory damages and $1,500,000 in punitive damages to Foote; and awarded $150,000 in compensatory damages and $1,000,000 in punitive damages to Africa House. The defendants filed a motion for new trial or remittitur, which the district court denied. The defendants also filed a motion for judgment as a matter of law. The district court granted this motion in part, finding that Foote's claims merged with those of Africa House and, therefore, she was without standing. The court dismissed Foote and set aside the verdict and damages in her favor. The plaintiffs filed an application for attorney fees pursuant to 42 U.S.C. § 1988(b). The district court granted this motion, but reduced the hourly rates requested. The district court further granted the plaintiffs' motion for prejudgment interest.

II.

We first address plaintiffs' contention that the district court erred in dismissing Foote's § 1981 and § 1982 claims for lack of standing. The district court reasoned that dismissal was necessary because the injury was suffered by Africa House rather than Foote, in that the defendants had refused to contract with or lease property to Africa House rather than to Foote individually, and that Foote's claim for injuries was the result of that refusal. The plaintiffs argue on appeal that Foote has standing because as sole shareholder of Africa House she suffered injury separate and distinct from that of Africa House, and further that she has standing in her own right because she signed a guaranty contract in her 1993 lease which gave rise to a special duty separate and distinct from that owed to Africa House.

We review issues of standing de novo. *Faustin v. City & County of Denver, Colorado*, 268 F.3d 942, 947 (10th Cir. 2001). In order to determine whether Foote has standing to claim injury under §1981 and § 1982, we first consider the language used in those statutes. Section 42 U.S.C. 1981 guarantees the right of all persons to "make and enforce" contracts. Section 42 U.S.C. 1982 guarantees the right to "inherit, purchase, lease, sell, hold, and convey real and personal property." It has been held that "[p] rudential limitations on standing ordinarily require that an action under section 1981 or 1982 be brought by the direct victims of the alleged discrimination because they are best situated to assert the individual rights in question." *Clifton Terrace Assocs., Ltd. v. United Technologies Corp.*, 929 F.2d 714, 721 (D.C. Cir. 1991).

In the instant case, Foote alleged discrimination based on her race. However, the party seeking to contract with the defendants and to lease property, and thus the direct victim of the alleged discrimination, was Foote's corporation, Africa House, rather than Foote herself.(1) We agree that Africa House has standing to assert discrimination claims under § 1981 and § 1982 where such discrimination is based on the race of one of its employees. *See Gersman v. Group Health Ass'n, Inc.*, 931 F.2d 1565 (D.C. Cir. 1991), *vacated on other grounds*, 502 U.S. 1068 (1992).(2) The question is whether Foote has standing to bring a claim for emotional damages which she herself allegedly suffered as a result of the defendants' discrimination.

We have held that, as a general rule, a stockholder cannot maintain a personal action against a third party for harm caused to the corporation. *Stat-Tech Intern. Corp. v. Delutes*, 47 F.3d 1054, 1060 (10th Cir. 1995). There is, however, an exception to this rule where the actions of the third party that injure the corporation also cause injury to the shareholder which is unique to himself or herself as a shareholder of the corporation and not suffered by the other shareholders. *Id.*

Foote alleged that she suffered emotional distress as a result of the defendants' actions. However, this distress arose from the failure of the defendants to contract with or lease to Africa House and was a product of the economic damages which were suffered by the corporation. Foote suffered no violation of her contract rights or right to lease that was in any way different from the violations claimed by Africa House. Her claim is derivative of that of Africa House and she does not have standing to sue on her own behalf. *See Bellows v. Amoco Oil Co.*, 118 F.3d 268, 276-77 (5th Cir. 1997) (holding that plaintiff who was president of a corporation and 51% shareholder had no individual cause of action under § 1981 for emotional distress arising from discrimination against the corporation based on plaintiff's race).

Foote also argues that she has standing as the result of her guarantee of the corporation's 1993 lease. However, we reject the premise that a stockholder's status as a guarantor gives the stockholder status to assert an individual claim against a third party where that harm is derivative of that suffered by the corporation. *See Sparling v. Hoffman Constr. Co.*, 864 F.2d 635, 640 (9th Cir. 1988); *Nicholson v. Ash*, 800 P.2d 1352, 1357 (Colo. App. 1990). Foote's status as guarantor of the previous lease is of no significance to her claim that the defendants refused to contract or lease to her corporation.

We hold that the district court did not err in dismissing Foote as an individual plaintiff and setting aside the damages awarded to her.

III.

We next consider the defendants' contention that their motion for judgment as a matter of law should have been granted because there was insufficient evidence to sustain the jury's finding of intentional race discrimination. In reviewing the district court's denial of a Rule 50(b) motion for judgment as a matter of law, we apply the same standard as the district court. *Tyler v. RE/MAX Mountain States, Inc.*, 232 F.3d 808, 812 (10th Cir. 2000). We review all the evidence in the record, construing it and all inferences drawn therefrom most favorably to the nonmoving party, and refrain from making credibility determinations or weighing the evidence. *Id.* A party is entitled to judgment as a matter of law only if there is no legally sufficient evidentiary basis for the claim. *Hampton v. Dillard Dept. Stores, Inc.*, 247

F.3d 1091, 1103 (10th Cir. 2001).

A § 1981 or § 1982 plaintiff must prove by a preponderance of the evidence that the defendant intentionally discriminated against him or her on the basis of race. *See Stewart v. Adolph Coors Co.*, 217 F.3d 1285, 1288 (10th Cir. 2000). Such proof may come from either direct or indirect evidence. *Hampton*, 247 F.3d at 1107. When asked to review the sufficiency of the evidence in §1981 and § 1982 claims based on indirect discrimination, we assume that the plaintiff met his or her burden of proving a prima facie claim and the claim properly went to trial, leaving only the question of whether the plaintiff presented sufficient evidence to support the jury's determination that the adverse action was taken on the basis of race. *Id.* at 1108; *Stewart*, 217 F.3d at 1288.

Based on the record as a whole, we conclude there was sufficient evidence from which a jury could infer that the defendants discriminated against Africa House. Although the undisputed evidence indicated that Africa House was always an excellent tenant at the Tabor Center, and although the defendants could not identify a legitimate reason why she would not be an appropriate tenant in the future, the defendants made no attempt to discuss the possibility of a future lease. The defendants told Foote that Africa House was not eligible for a long-term lease because it did not have enough gross annual sales; however, at the same time they offered a long-term lease to another business whose year-to-date sales were approximately $20,000 less and whose rent-to-sales ratio was comparable. When Foote attempted to pursue a short-term lease, she was told that spaces were unavailable or was begrudgingly offered only a temporary lease even though, at the same time, the defendants were soliciting other tenants for short-term leases. At one point, the defendants made misrepresentations to Foote concerning why they were taking measurements of her business, telling her the measurements were for insurance purposes when they were actually in preparation for a new tenant.

Further, there is evidence from which a jury could infer that Foote's race and the perceived race of Africa House's clientele were the basis for this discriminatory conduct. There was testimony from Jana Thorpe, a tenant who was offered a long-term lease, that when she asked whether Foote's business would be offered a long-term lease, she was told that the business "didn't fit the proposed image of the Tabor Center." App. at 1343. She interpreted this statement to mean that "Africa House didn't fit the image of the Tabor Center [because] Africa House was a store owned by a black person that sold things from Africa and had black customers." *Id.* at 1344. There was also testimony that Yarmouth management told Foote that her business did not "mix well," was not glamourous enough, and devalued the Center, while at the same time tenants who were not black were encouraged to sign leases. Further, management stated at various times that the name "Africa House" should be changed.

Reviewing the evidence presented at trial, we cannot say that "the evidence points but one way, and is susceptible to no reasonable inferences supporting [the plaintiffs'] claim." *Hampton*, 247 F.3d at 1107. The district court did not err in denying the defendants' motion for judgment as a matter of law based on the sufficiency of the evidence.

IV.

The defendants next contend there was insufficient evidence to support the jury's determination that they interfered with Africa House's prospective business advantages, and that the district court erred in denying their motion for judgment as a matter of law as to that claim. They argue that Africa House failed to introduce evidence that the defendants induced or otherwise caused a third person not to enter into or continue a prospective business relationship.

After a careful review of the record, we are unable to find any evidence to support the jury's verdict. On appeal, Africa House similarly fails to point to any evidence which would support the verdict. As a result, we reverse the jury's verdict on this issue.

V.

The defendants next argue that the district court committed several trial errors which, individually and cumulatively, require reversal. "When a party seeks 'reversal of a jury verdict or of a denial of a motion for new trial' by claiming trial errors, it 'must establish the alleged trial errors were both prejudicial and clearly erroneous.'" *Baty v. Willamette Indus., Inc.*, 172 F.3d 1232, 1247 (10th Cir. 1999) (quoting *Gust v. Jones*, 162 F.3d 587, 591 (10th Cir. 1998)).

First, defendants assert that it was error for the district court to allow the lay opinion testimony of three witnesses: Jana Thorpe, Phil Pankoff, and David Fine. Under Federal Rule of Evidence 701, lay opinion must be "(a) rationally based on the perception of the witness, and (b) helpful to a clear understanding of the witness' testimony or the determination of a fact in issue." The admission of lay opinion testimony is within the sound discretion of the district court. *Gust*, 162 F.3d at 595. We conclude that the district court did not abuse its discretion in admitting the testimony. The testimony of Thorpe, Pankoff and Fine was rationally based on their perceptions and helpful to a determination of facts in issue.

The defendants also argue that the district court erred in denying their motions in limine seeking to exclude (1) the plaintiffs' expert witness, Dr. William Kaempfer, and (2) irrelevant comparative evidence. The district court denied the motions, reserving the issues for trial. At trial, the defendants did not object to any of the testimony identified in their motions in limine. As a result, they have failed to preserve these alleged errors for appeal. *See Hampton*, 247 F.3d at 1113 (stating that failure to make a timely and proper objection constitutes waiver of the issue absent plain error resulting in manifest injustice). We conclude that the defendants have failed to show the denial of their motions in limine resulted in manifest injustice.

The defendants further contend that the district court abused its discretion when it granted the plaintiffs' motion in limine to exclude a finding made by the Colorado Civil Rights Commission that there was no cause to believe that the defendants had discriminated against the plaintiffs in the leasing decision. However, the decision of whether to admit or exclude findings of a civil rights commission lies within the sound discretion of the district court. *See Denny v. Hutchinson Sales Corp.*, 649 F.2d 816, 821-22 (10th Cir. 1981). The defendants sought to admit the finding on the grounds that it might contain statements to the commission that would contradict Foote's testimony at trial. The district court excluded the evidence, but stated that it would entertain a motion for reconsideration in the event that Foote actually did make statements at trial that conflicted with her testimony to the commission. The defendants made no attempt to do so, and do not now point to any conflicting statements. The district court did not abuse its discretion in granting the plaintiffs' motion in limine to exclude the commission report.

The defendants next argue that the district court erred when it allowed plaintiffs' counsel, during closing argument, to refer to the size and scope of the defendants' operations. Plaintiffs' counsel implored the jury to "send a clear message" "all the way to Sydney, Australia where [the defendants] are based on the other side of the world," and further implied that the large size, international operations, and presumed profitability of the defendants warranted a large award of punitive damages. App. at 1725-27. However, the defendants did not object to this statement at closing argument, and we will not address it on appeal. *See Glenn v. Cessna Aircraft Co.*, 32 F.3d 1462, 1465 (10th Cir. 1994) (holding that "[a] party who waits until the jury returns an unfavorable verdict to complain about improper comments during opening statement and closing argument is bound by that risky decision and should not be granted relief")

Finally, the defendants contend that the district court erred in allowing Foote to remain as a plaintiff in the case. They argue that her presence in the case confused the jury. However, at no time during trial did the defendants object to Foote's presence as a plaintiff. Under the circumstances, there was no error.

VI.

We next consider the defendants' argument that the compensatory damages awarded to Africa House were not supported by sufficient evidence. The jury was instructed that, in determining compensatory damages, it could consider (1) financial losses, including lost profits and expenses; and (2) loss of good name, reputation, honor or integrity. The jury ultimately awarded $150,000 in compensatory damages.

We will uphold a jury's award of damages unless it is clearly erroneous or there is no evidence to support the award. *See Brown v. Presbyterian Healthcare Services*, 101 F.3d 1324, 1330 (10th Cir. 1996). "[T]he amount of damages awarded by a jury can be supported by any competent evidence tending to sustain it." *Advantor Capital Corp. v. Yeary*, 136 F.3d 1259, 1266 (10th Cir. 1998) (quoting *Bennett v. Longácre*, 774 F.2d 1024, 1028 (10th Cir. 1985)).

Dr. William Kaempfer testified as to Africa House's lost profits, ultimately fixing the lost profits as a result of the defendants' conduct at $75,316.95. The defendants argue that this testimony was unreliable. However, the jury apparently found the testimony credible. "It is within the virtually exclusive purview of the jury to evaluate credibility and fix damages." *United Intern. Holdings v. Wharf (Holdings)*, 210 F.3d 1207, 1230 (10th Cir. 2000). Thus, Dr. Kaempfer's testimony was sufficient to support $75,316.95 in compensatory damages.

We do not, however, reach the same conclusion regarding the remaining $74,683.05 in compensatory damages awarded by the jury. The plaintiffs contend that the award is supported by the testimony of Andrew Warren, Lewis Gaiter, Kathleen Scheuerman, and Foote herself. However, while financial consultants Warren and Gaiter suggested new business strategies which would help Africa House increase its business, most of these business strategies were not adopted, and in fact the suggestions were made more than one year prior to the alleged actions of the defendants. They expressed no opinion concerning lost profits or loss of Africa House's good name, honor or integrity. Similarly, Kathleen Scheuerman, an employee of Africa House, testified only that the business in the new space was not as profitable as it was in the old space, and her testimony in no way supports an award for lost profits above that presented by Dr. Kaempfer, nor does it provide any evidence of a loss of good name, reputation, honor or integrity.

Finally, Foote's testimony fails to support lost profits over and above those calculated by her expert, and does not mention any damage to Africa House's good name, reputation, honor, or integrity. As a result, we conclude there is insufficient evidence to sustain a compensatory damage award over and above $75,316.95, and remand with directions that the district court enter a remittitur reducing the compensatory damages awarded to Africa House to that amount or, in the alternative, order a new trial.

VII.

The defendants contend that the district court erred in denying their motion for judgment as a matter of law, arguing the punitive damages awarded to Africa House are not supported by the evidence.[3]

"Whether sufficient evidence exists to support punitive damages is a question of law reviewed de novo." *Fitzgerald v. Mountain States Tel. & Tel. Co.*, 68 F.3d 1257, 1262 (10th Cir. 1995). We have held that the standard for punitive damages in actions claiming a violation of federal civil rights requires that the discrimination must have been malicious, willful, and in gross disregard of the rights of the plaintiff. *See Hampton*, 247 F.3d at 1115.

We conclude that this standard for punitive damages cannot be satisfied by a showing of intentional discrimination alone. Otherwise, every jury verdict in a successful § 1981 or § 1982 claim would include an award of punitive damages. Instead, we believe that a plaintiff must prove that the defendant acted with malicious, willful or gross disregard of a plaintiff's rights over and above intentional discrimination.

In examining the evidence, we are not persuaded that the plaintiffs proved the defendants acted in malicious, willful or gross disregard of their rights. While the indirect evidence in this case is sufficient to establish that the defendants intentionally discriminated against the plaintiffs on the basis of race, there is no evidence which would show that the defendants acted in malicious or willful disregard of Africa House's rights. As a result, we reverse the district court's denial of the defendants' motion for judgment as a matter of law as to the $1 million in punitive damages awarded to Africa House.

VIII.

The defendants next contend that the district court abused its discretion when it applied a state law rate of interest to compute the award of prejudgment interest to Africa House. The district court applied a 9% interest rate to the prejudgment interest award pursuant to Colo. Rev. Stat. Ann. § 13-21-101. The defendants argue that the district court should have applied the rate of interest for post-judgment awards found in 28 U.S.C. § 1961 because the district court's jurisdiction was based on a federal question jurisdiction rather than diversity jurisdiction.

We agree that a federal rate of interest rather than the state rate applies where jurisdiction is based on a federal question, and therefore the district court erred in determining that it was bound to apply the state rate of interest. *See Carpenters Dist. Council of New Orleans & Vicinity v. Dillard Dept. Stores, Inc.*, 15 F.3d 1275, 1288 (5th Cir. 1994) (stating that "federal law governs the range of remedies, including the allowance and rate of prejudgment interest, where a cause of action, as in this case, arises out of federal statute"). *See also U.S. Industries, Inc. v. Touche Ross & Co.*, 854 F.2d 1223, 1254 (10th Cir. 1988) (stating that an award of prejudgment interest in a federal securities law claim is controlled by federal law), *overruled by implication on other grounds by Central Bank of Denver v. First Interstate Bank of Denver*, 511 U.S. 164 (1994). We therefore remand to the district court to fix the rate of prejudgment interest. *See Towerridge, Inc. v. T.A.O., Inc.*, 111 F.3d 758, 764 (10th Cir. 1997) (stating where the prejudgment rate is governed by federal law, a court is free to choose any rate which would fairly compensate the plaintiff for the delay); *see also Jones v. Unum Life Ins. Co. of America*, 223 F.3d 130, 139 (2d Cir. 2000) (holding that because there is no federal statute that purports to control the rate of prejudgment interest, the rate is left to the discretion of the district court).

The defendants also contend that the district court erred in awarding prejudgment interest from the date that the claim accrued rather than as the lost profits occurred. They argue that because the lost profits did not all occur at the time the claim accrued, awarding prejudgment interest from the date the claim accrued gives a windfall to the plaintiffs.

The purpose of prejudgment interest is "'to compensate the wronged party for being deprived of the monetary value of his loss from the time of the loss to the payment of judgment.'" *Anixter v. Home-Stake Prod. Co.*, 977 F.2d 1549, 1554 (10th Cir. 1992) (quoting *U.S. Industries*, 854 F.2d at 1256). It appears that the district court in the case at hand may have felt bound to apply state law found in Colo. Rev. Stat. Ann. § 13-21-101 to the calculation of prejudgment interest, which provides for prejudgment interest to be calculated from the date the action accrued. On remand, we direct the district court to consider the timing of the award of prejudgment interest that will serve to fairly compensate Africa House for the deprivation of the monetary value of its loss.

IX.

The plaintiffs also contend that the district court erred in reducing the rates at which attorney fees were calculated for purposes of its award under 42 U.S.C. § 1988(b). The plaintiffs had requested fees for a total of 482.70 hours by attorney Darold Killmer at $250 per hour, 309.55 hours by attorney David Miller at $250 per hour, and 118.60 hours by attorney Mari Newman at $115 per hour. The district court reduced Killmer's and Miller's hourly rates to $200 and reduced Newman's hourly rate to $100, finding that the plaintiffs had failed to produce evidence showing that the higher rates were reasonable.

"In light of the discretionary nature of the district court's decision, we review an attorney's fee award under 42 U.S.C. § 1988(b) for an abuse of discretion." *Robinson v. City of Edmond*, 160 F.3d 1275, 1280 (10th Cir. 1998). We review the district court's factual findings for clear error, and the court's legal conclusions de novo. *Id.*

A claimant who files an application for attorney fees under § 1988(b) has the burden to prove that the fee is reasonable. *Id.* A reasonable rate is the prevailing market rate in the relevant community. *Malloy v. Monahan*, 73 F.3d 1012, 1018 (10th Cir. 1996). To meet this burden, the claimant must:

produce satisfactory evidence - in addition to the attorney's own affidavits - that the requested rates are in line with those prevailing in the community for similar services by lawyers of reasonably comparable skill, experience and reputation. A rate determined in this way is normally deemed to be reasonable and is referred to - for convenience - as the prevailing market rate.

Blum v. Stenson, 465 U.S. 886, 895 n. 11 (1984).

Here, the evidence fails to show that the requested rates were reasonable. While Killmer submitted an affidavit as to the prevailing rates at his firm and another local firm, the rates charged by attorneys at the other firm ranged from only $160 to $190 per hour. An affidavit from Lynn Feiger, a former partner of Killmer, stated only that she charged $310 per hour for the same type of work. While this evidence serves to establish Feiger's rate, it does not establish the rates charged were consistent with rates charged by comparably skilled lawyers in the community. Similarly, the only evidence of the appropriateness of Newman's hourly rate was provided in the affidavit of Killmer.

The defendants contend that, instead of relying on their asserted rates, the district court incorrectly relied on its own knowledge. However, we are unpersuaded by this argument. Where a district court does not have before it adequate evidence of prevailing market rates, the court may use other relevant factors, including its own knowledge, to establish the rate. *See Case v. Unified Sch. Dist. No. 233*, 157 F.3d 1243 (10th Cir. 1998). We conclude that the district court did not err in finding that the plaintiffs failed to satisfy their burden of establishing the reasonableness of the requested attorney fees and in reducing those rates according to its own knowledge of the prevailing market rate.

X.

The decision of the district court dismissing Foote for lack of standing is AFFIRMED. We VACATE the judgment and direct the district court to dismiss Africa House's claim of intentional interference with prospective business advantages. We REVERSE the district court's denial of the defendants' request for a remittitur and REMAND with directions that the district court enter a remittitur order reducing the compensatory damages awarded to Africa House to $75,316.95 or, in the alternative, to grant a new trial. We AFFIRM the district court's denial of the defendants' motion for a new trial for alleged evidentiary errors. We REVERSE the district court's denial of the defendants' motion for judgment as a matter of law as to the punitive damages awarded to Africa House and VACATE the award of punitive damages. We REVERSE the district court's order granting prejudgment interest at the state rate from the date the claim accrued, and REMAND for a determination of the rate of prejudgment interest and for a determination of the date or dates of accrual. We AFFIRM the district court's award of attorney fees.

Nos. 99-1388 et al., The Guides v. The Yarmouth Group

JENKINS, Senior District Judge, concurring and dissenting.

I concur with the majority opinion with one modest exception. I would reverse the order of the court below dismissing Ms. Foote's jury award and reinstate her compensatory damages judgment of $200,000.

Section 1981 states that "[a]ll persons . . . shall have the same right . . . to make and enforce contracts . . . as is enjoyed by white citizens." 42 U.S.C. § 1981 (1994). Section 1982 states that "[a]ll citizens of the United States shall have the same right . . . as is enjoyed by white citizens thereof to inherit, purchase, lease, sell, hold, and convey real and personal property." 42 U.S.C. § 1982 (1994). Initially enacted pursuant to the Civil Rights Act of 1866, sections 1981 and 1982 were "intended [to protect] . . . citizens of the United States in enjoyment of certain rights without discrimination on account of race, color, or previous condition of servitude," United States v. Cruikshank, 92 U.S. 542, 555 (1875), or because of their ancestry or ethnic characteristics, St. Francis College v. Al-Khazraji, 481 U.S. 604 (1987), and to "confer on [African-Americans] a civil status equivalent to that enjoyed by white persons." Valle v. Stengel, 176 F.2d 697, 703 (3d Cir. 1949). The protection afforded by these statutes finds its roots in the Thirteenth and Fourteenth Amendments. See Runyon v. McCrary, 427 U.S. 160, 16872 (1976) (Thirteenth Amendment); Jones v. Alfred H. Mayer Co., 392 U.S. 409, 43744 (1968) (same); General Bldg. Contractors Ass'n v. Pennsylvania, 458 U.S. 375, 38491 (1982) (Fourteenth Amendment).

Although neither section 1981 or 1982 define "person" or "citizen," respectively, the United States Supreme Court has provided useful guidance. In Arlington Heights v. Metropolitan Housing Development Corporation, 429 U.S. 252 (1977), the Court stated that, for the purposes of standing under the Fourteenth Amendment, "a corporation . . . has no racial identity and cannot be the direct target of the . . . alleged discrimination." Id. at 263.

In today's opinion, the majority disregards Arlington Heights in concluding that Africa House has standing because under sections 1981 and 1982, "the direct victim of the alleged discrimination, was Foote's corporation, Africa House, rather than Foote herself."

In this case, Africa House by itself cannot have standing to assert section 1981 and 1982 claims because, as Arlington Heights explains, a corporation cannot be the direct target or victim of racial discrimination. However, the Court in Arlington Heights did not address whether a corporation would have standing if it were an indirect target of racial discrimination, that is, whether a corporation has standing when it suffers an injury such as lost profits resulting from unlawful discrimination directed at a member of a protected class. Cases since Arlington Heights indicate that a corporation that is harmed by discriminatory action has standing to litigate that harm. See Hudson Valley Freedom Theater, Inc. v. Heimbach, 671 F.2d 702, 708 (2d Cir. 1982) (Pierce, J., concurring) ("[U]nder the 14th Amendment and the statutes which seek to implement its purposes, any person, including a colorless corporate 'person', although not a member of a protected group, has an implied cause of action against any other person who, with racially discriminatory intent, causes . . . it . . . [an] injury."). This view comports with the Court's dictum in Arlington Heights and the purposes for which Congress enacted sections 1981 and 1982.

The majority relies on Gersman v. Group Health Association, Inc., 931 F.2d 1565 (D.C. Cir. 1991), *vacated on other grounds*, 502 U.S. 1068 (1992), to hold that "Africa House has standing to assert discrimination claims under § 1981 and § 1982 where such discrimination is based on the race of one of its employees."

I agree with the reasoning in Gersman,[(1)] and I agree that the jury correctly found that Africa House suffered an injury resulting from unlawful discrimination. However, the jury also found that the defendants had discriminated against Ms. Foote because of her race and that Ms. Foote suffered a compensable injury distinct from that suffered by Africa House.[(2)] Ms. Foote, as is required by our prior cases,[(3)] is a member of the protected class under sections 1981 and 1982 and was the direct target of the defendants' racial discrimination whether she was acting in her individual capacity in seeking to enter into the prospective lease contract,[(4)] or was acting as agent for her corporation. She is entitled to redress for her own injuries that also fall clearly within the zone of interests protected by sections 1981 and 1982. The defendants caused injury both to Africa House and Ms. Foote by refusing to deal with Ms. Foote--a refusal the jury found to be racially motivated. Affirming the defendants' liability to the corporate plaintiff, Africa House, acknowledges that the corporation suffered an injury resulting from unlawful discrimination--racial discrimination for which Ms. Foote served as the very human direct target.

In dismissing Ms. Foote's claims, the majority relies on Bellows v. Amoco Oil Company, 118 F.3d 268 (5th Cir. 1997). However, Bellows does not support the majority's holding for several reasons. First, in Bellows, the jury found in favor of the defendant Amoco on the corporate plaintiff's section 1981 claim. The corporate plaintiff, Phillips Industrial Constructors, Inc. ("PICI"), did not appeal the jury's determination and was therefore not before the Fifth Circuit at all. As the court itself stated: "The obvious problem that Bellow faces with [his] argument, of course, is that the jury found that Amoco did not interfere with PICI's contracts, or ability to contract, with Amoco on the basis of race." Id. at 276. In other words, the court found that Bellow's claim, as it was dependent on PICI's dismissed claim against Amoco, was meritless on appeal. Second, the facts are distinguishable from the facts of the present case in that Bellow's claim was one step removed from the cause of action as expressed by PICI. That is, in Bellows, plaintiff Bellow claimed that Amoco discriminated against him on the basis of his race by engaging in conduct that had the effect of terminating, modifying, or changing Bellow's right to contract with PICI as distinguished from PICI's right to contract with Amoco. Id. at 27273.

Ms. Foote is not asserting that the defendants interfered with her right to contract with Africa House. Ms. Foote is asserting that she has an injury resulting directly from the defendants' discriminatory conduct towards her, separate and distinct from that suffered by Africa House--an issue not raised or dealt with in Bellows or Gersman. Rather than her claim being "derivative of that of Africa House," if anything, Africa House's claim is derivative of the unlawful discrimination Ms. Foote experienced firsthand in dealing with the defendants. Africa House could make no contract without her participation. The jury found that the defendants frustrated Ms. Foote's efforts to obtain a new lease, and did so because of Ms. Foote's race, thereby harming both Ms. Foote and Africa House.

The majority dismisses Ms. Foote's harm as merely "a product of the economic damages which were suffered by the corporation." Yet the uncontroverted testimony of Ms. Foote and other witnesses established that she became deeply disturbed beginning in September 1996--before Africa House had suffered any actual economic loss. The jury found in Ms. Foote's favor, awarding her $200,000 in damages.

The majority has simply substituted its judgment for that of the jury concerning whether Ms. Foote suffered the mental anguish that she and others testified to at trial as resulting from the discrimination she experienced.

I would therefore hold that both Africa House and Ms. Foote have standing to assert the section 1981 and 1982 causes of action against the defendants, and that the district court's ruling as to Ms. Foote should be reversed and judgment in favor of Ms. Foote should be reinstated as to compensatory damages.

FOOTNOTES

Click footnote number to return to corresponding location in the text.

*. The Yarmouth Group Property Management, Inc., is now known as Jones Lang LaSalle Property Management, Inc.

2. The Honorable Bruce S. Jenkins, United States Senior District Judge for the District of Utah, sitting by designation.

1. According to the Stipulated Pretrial Order, the plaintiffs' claims with regard to § 1981 and § 1982 are that "defendants have denied The Africa House the opportunity to rent or negotiate for the rental of retail space at The Shops at Tabor Center." App. at 61. The complaint identifies Africa House as the corporation. *Id.* at 36.

2. In *Gersman*, a corporation, CSI, brought a § 1981 claim against a defendant who had ended a contractual relationship when the defendant learned that the president of CSI was Jewish. The court held that CSI had standing to bring suit under § 1981 because the injury it suffered fell "within the zone of interests protected by the statute," in that the termination of the contract was "solely because an individual associated with CSI was Jewish." 931 F.2d at 1569. *See also Hudson Valley Freedom Theater, Inc. v. Heimbach*, 671 F.2d 702, 706 (2d Cir. 1982) (holding theater corporation had standing to assert claim alleging it was discriminated against because it sought to involve the black and Hispanic communities).

3. The plaintiffs argue that defendants failed to raise the issue of insufficient evidence to support punitive damages in their Fed. R. Civ. P. 50(a) motions, and therefore should not have been allowed to raise the issue in a Fed R. Civ. P. 50(b) motion, or on appeal. However, the plaintiffs themselves failed to object on this basis in their response to the defendants' Rule 50(b) motion. Under such circumstances, the plaintiffs may not assert the failure of the defendants to raise the insufficient evidence issue. When the non-moving party fails to raise the inadequacy of a Rule 50(a) motion in opposition to a Rule 50(b) motion, that party cannot raise waiver as an argument on appeal. *See Williams v. Runyon*, 130 F.3d 568, 572 (3d Cir. 1997); *Thompson & Wallace of Memphis, Inc. v. Falconwood Corp.*, 100 F.3d 429, 435 (5th Cir. 1996); *Whelan v. Abell*, 48 F.3d 1247, 1251-53 (D.C. Cir. 1995); *Gibeau v. Nellis*, 18 F.3d 107, 109 (2d Cir. 1994); *Collins v. Illinois*, 830 F.2d 692, 698 (7th Cir. 1987); *Beauford v. Sisters of Mercy Province of Detroit, Inc.*, 816 F.2d 1104, 1108 n.3 (6th Cir. 1987); *Halsell v. Kimberly Clark Corp.*, 683 F.2d 285, 293-95 (8th Cir. 1982). Therefore, we will address the issue.

[1] Gersman adequately addresses the difficult issues raised in Arlington Heights. In Gersman, the defendant argued that the corporation, CSI, did not have standing to bring a cause of action under section 1981 because CSI lacked a racial or religious identity. Gersman, 931 F.2d at 1568. The court declined to rule that "racial identity is a predicate to discriminatory harm" and instead approached the issue "by assuming that, if a corporation can suffer harm from discrimination, it has standing to litigate that harm." Id. Addressing this issue further, the court stated

a party may suffer a legally cognizable injury from discrimination even where that party is not a member of a protected minority group. Thus, it is not necessary to determine whether CSI has a "racial identity." [Given that a corporation exists as an entity separate from its employees, officers and stockholders,] [s]uch a query would lead to difficulties of determining what, in fact, constitutes a racial identity. . . . For example, in the present case, CSI alleges that it has a racial identity because it is operated and owned by Mr. and Mrs. Gersman, who are both Jewish. Yet the situation would be no different if Gentile shareholders owned CSI and [the defendant] ended the contractual relationship because the corporation had a single Jewish employee. Thus, CSI need not have a "Jewish identity," or even have predominantly Jewish owners or employees, in order to suffer injury from [the defendant's] discriminatory actions.

Id. at 1570.

[2] The jury was instructed:

If you find that either or both of the Defendants discriminated on the basis of Plaintiffs' race in the making or enforcement of a lease for the Tabor Center for which they were qualified, you may award reasonable compensation for the following:

financial losses (for either Plaintiff Tseghe Foote or Plaintiff Africa House);

pain, suffering, and physical and emotional distress (for Plaintiff Tseghe Foote only).

. . .

If you find for the Plaintiffs, or either of them, on more than one claim for relief, you may award damages only once for the same business losses.

(Jt. App. vol. I-A, at 308, 310.)

[3] In this Circuit, a racial identity is the cornerstone of a section 1981 and 1982 cause of action and a necessary element of a plaintiff's prima facie case. See Shawl v. Dillards, Inc., No. 99-1409, 2001 WL 967887, at *2 (10th Cir. Aug. 27, 2001) ("To establish a claim under § 1981, the plaintiffs must show that (1) they are members of a protected class . . . ." (citing Hampton v. Dillard Dep't Stores, Inc., 247 F.3d 1091, 1101 (10th Cir.2001))).

[4] The majority bases its holding that the corporation was the direct victim of the alleged discrimination, in part, on the fact that the injury--the refusal to contract with or lease property--was suffered by Africa House, not Ms. Foote individually. However, the majority ignores evidence in the record that suggests that Ms. Foote leased space from the defendants under her own name, "Tseghe Foote, Tenant." On the existing record, whether Africa House was to be the party to the prospective contract is ambiguous at best. (Jt. App. vol. X, at 244549.)

10th | Keyword | Case | Docket | Date: Filed / Added | WP (78480 bytes) RTF (64663 bytes)

Comments to: WebMaster, ca10@law.wuacc.edu.
Updated: July 3, 2002.
HTML markup Copyright © 2002, Washburn University School of Law.
URL: http://lawdns.wuacc.edu/ca10/cases/2002/07/99-1388.htm.

KILLMER & LANE, LLP ATTORNEYS AT LAW

1543 CHAMPA ST. • SUITE 400 • THE ODD FELLOWS HALL • DENVER, CO 80202
303.571.1000 • FAX: 303.571.1001 • www.killmerlane.com

DAROLD W. KILLMER
DAVID A. LANE
MARI NEWMAN

February 20, 2003

Hand Delivered

Judge Robbie M. Barr
JUDICIAL ARBITER GROUP, INC.
1601 Blake Street, Suite 400
Denver, CO 80202

Re: *Africa House v. Tabor Center Mediation*
JAG Number: 03-179

Dear Judge Barr:

This letter and package of materials is submitted to help you prepare for next week's mediation in the above-captioned case. We are very pleased that you have agreed to serve as a Mediator in this very important case.

As more fully explained in this letter, we are willing to settle this case in exchange for payments aggregating to $1,565,000.

INTRODUCTION

This much has been judicially established, and is not subject to any further dispute: the owners and property managers of the Tabor Center shopping center in Denver, Colorado illegally discriminated against one of its finest tenants, Africa House, when it attempted to evict the store from its premises and, having failed in its attempt to evict, transferred the store from an attractive third-floor location to a far less attractive second floor location. Sixteen different people have been legally charged with answering the question of whether Defendants' conduct in this regard constituted illegal race discrimination: twelve jurors, trial judge Daniel Sparr, and three judges on the Tenth Circuit Court of Appeals. **All sixteen** have agreed that Defendants illegally discriminated against Africa House.

The only question remaining to be resolved, then, is one of damages and attorney fees. It is our hope that these issues can be resolved at next week's mediation.

Judge Robbie Barr
February 20, 2003
Page (5)

occupied by Africa House prior to the illegal racially discriminatory transfer, GNC Foods, operated continuously in that very attractive space, and continues to operate there today. Notably, the addition of ESPN SportsZone to the third floor has generated increased foot traffic which serves to benefit the businesses nearby, including the GNC store which occupies Africa House's old space.

In other words, Defendants' discriminatory transfer of Africa House to a much more vulnerable location had the foreseeable effect of causing it to go out of business in July 2001 when that part of the shopping center closed for renovations. The discriminatory transfer thus caused substantial economic losses to Africa House, almost all of them occurring after the October 1, 1999 cutoff of Dr. Kaempfer's earlier economic analysis.

2. Africa House's Economic Losses Are Substantial

As reflected by Dr. Kaempfer's updated damages report, Africa House's economic losses are considerably higher than they were at the time of the trial in 1999. Dr. Kaempfer's report reflects losses ranging from $510,176 to $930,176 resulting from Africa House's forced relocation and subsequent closure.

3. Attorneys Fees and Costs

Africa House is entitled to receive its attorney fees and costs as the "prevailing party" in this civil rights litigation. While there has already been a partial award of fees (covering the period through August 2, 1999), and that award was affirmed on appeal by the Tenth Circuit Court of Appeals, such award provides only the starting point for the analysis.

a. Attorneys Fees are Calculated at Current Rates

First, it is well established that the award requires recalculation at current hourly rates, rather than historical hourly rates, to compensate for the significant delay in payment. It has long been the law in this Circuit that "[t]he hourly rate at which compensation is awarded should reflect rates in effect at the time the fee is being established by the court, rather than those in effect at the time the services were performed. The lawyers seeking fees usually will not have been paid for their services until the court makes its allowance. We think that awarding compensation at current rates will roughly approximate periodic compensation adjusted for inflation and interest and will obviate the necessity of guessing when periodic billings would have been made and paid in an analogous private practice situation." *Ramos v. Lamm*, 713 F.2d 546, 555 (10th Cir. 1983). The Tenth Circuit's wisdom on this matter was confirmed by the United

Apr 13 05 03:23p LeHouillier & Associates 17194733292 p.2

04/13/2005 12:37 3033229546 THE BROCK HOUSE PAGE 02/03

DISTRICT COURT, COUNTY OF DENVER STATE OF COLORADO Court Address: Denver City and County Building 1437 Bannock Street, Room 256 Denver, CO 80202	▲COURT USE ONLY▲
TSEGHE FOOTE and THE GUIDES, LTD. d/b/a THE AFRICA HOUSE, Plaintiffs, v. MILLER, LANE, KILLMER & GREISEN, LLP; DAVID H. MILLER; DAROLD W. KILLMER; and KILLMER & LANE, LLP, Defendants.	Case Number: 2004 CV 1256 Courtroom: 5
Charles Welton Attorney for Plaintiff Attorney Registration #5337 1800 Gaylord Street Denver, CO 80206 Phone Number: (303) 333-9800 Facsimile Number: (303) 322-9546	

AFFIDAVIT OF PATRIC J. LEHOUILLIER

STATE OF COLORADO)
) ss.
County)

I, Patric J. LeHouillier, of lawful and being first duly sworn, state as follows:

1. I am and at all pertinent times have been duly licensed to practice law within the State of Colorado and actively engaged in the private practice of law in both Colorado Springs and Denver, Colorado. I presently do, and at all pertinent times have,

000505

included civil rights litigation within my practice. I am familiar with the standards of care and standards of conduct applicable to the Defendants in their representation of the Plaintiffs in the action which is underlying this legal malpractice claim.

2. I was asked to perform consulting services for Mr. Welton relative to the representation by the Defendants of the Plaintiffs in the underlying action. I have reviewed extensive materials in that regard. I have formulated opinions that the Defendants in their representation of the Plaintiffs in the underlying action failed to meet the applicable standards of care and standards of conduct. I have generated two (2) written reports, my initial report of February 9, 2004 and my supplemental report of February 2, 2005. I withdraw that portion of my opinion relating to a failure to object to an untimely filing of a 50(b) Motion in the underlying case. With that exception, the reports set forth my opinions held to a reasonable degree of probability supporting my conclusions that the Defendants failed to meet the above-referenced standards and the factual bases upon which those opinions are based.

Further, affiant sayeth not.

Patric J. LeHouillier

Subscribed and sworn to before me this 13th day of April, 2005, by Patric J. LeHouillier.

Witness my hand and official seal.

My commission expires: 9/30/2008.

(SEAL)

Notary Public

CHARLES WELTON P.C.
RECEIVED FEB 10 2004

LeHOUILLIER
& ASSOCIATES

ATTORNEYS AT LAW
PATRIC J. LeHOUILLIER*
*Also Admitted In New York

90 SOUTH CASCADE
SUITE 1480
COLORADO SPRINGS, COLORADO 80903-1619
TELEPHONE 719 471-1330
FAX 719 473-3292

February 9, 2004

Charles Welton, Esq.
The Brock House
1800 Gaylord Street
Denver, CO 80206

Re: Foote & The Africa House v. Killmer et al.

Dear Mr. Welton:

At your request, I have reviewed a considerable volume of data in this case. By no means, have I looked at everything in the nineteen boxes which Mr. Killmer had sent over, I have, however, looked at most of the pleadings and correspondence. I have also reviewed selected portions of the trial transcript and certain deposition transcripts. And, last but not least, I have had the occasion to confer with Ms. Foote and yourself in your office. Based on this review, I am willing to give my preliminary thoughts regarding the contemplated professional liability action against Mr. Darold W. Killmer and David H. Miller.

I.
FEE-RELATED ISSUES

At the outset, I would observe that fee-related issues ordinarily involve fiduciary questions as opposed to standard of care concerns. In essence, fiduciary breaches amount to violations of standards of conduct as opposed to substandard care which is the central liability question in a typical professional negligence action.

The tendering of a fee agreement by an attorney to his prospective client always presents a unique challenge. Often, the fee agreement is not presented until after the client actually believes that the lawyer is already representing him or her. Certainly, that was the situation here since Mr. Fine had already sent a withdrawal notice, having been notified by Mr. Killmer that his office was taking over the then Plaintiff's representation.

I am particularly troubled by the attorney's conduct in requesting the client's signature at the same time he presented the fee agreement to her on January 3, 1997.

Contrary to Mr. Killmer's subsequent representations to Judge Sparr, this Fee Agreement was not a stock Chapter 23.3 agreement. It was an agreement requiring the client to pay both $1,000.00 per quarter and 35 % of the gross recovery.

According to Ms. Foote, when the fee agreement was presented to her, the $1,000.00 quarterly obligation was explained in the context of her desire to retain her original Tabor Center space. Although the Fee Agreement itself discusses optional arrangements, Ms. Foote has indicated that no options were ever explained to her; she believed the fee agreement which was being presented was pretty much a "take it or leave" proposition. She was impressed by Mr. Killmer and very anxious to have her case progress. She signed the fee agreement at the same meeting at which is was presented.

According to Ms. Foote, the fee issue was revisited at the time of a Settlement Conference sometime after the fee agreement was executed. During this conference, Mr. Killmer was advocating that his clients accept the sum of $100,000.00 as an agreed upon settlement figure. Ms. Foote wanted no part of this; what she had wanted all along was the renewal of her lease and a promise to keep her in her original space at the Tabor Center. Since lawyer and client were not "on the same page" with respect to settlement objectives, Ms. Foote made it clear to Mr. Killmer that she thought he wanted a cash settlement to increase his fee. She further made it clear that she would be willing to pay him on an hourly basis if he would continue to represent her and assure that her interests were being promoted in the way that she was advocating. Mr. Killmer did not accept this offer from his clients. Settlement discussions broke down and later the case went to trial.

I had earlier mentioned that the Fee Agreement does not comport with Chapter 23.3. The costs estimate was exceeded by the firm without any written advice to the clients regarding additional costs and certainly without any written consent by the clients to the firm to incur additional costs.

The billings generated by the firm are confusing and inconsistent. At times, the $1,000.00 per quarter fee was assessed. At other times, it was not included in the billing statements. Similarly, "interest" charges were included on certain bills and excluded on others. Most disturbing in the context of the firm's billing records is the fact that there was no disbursement statement submitted to the client. By the time the $525,000.00 settlement was negotiated, there had been a major break in the attorney/client relationship. This does not excuse, however, the firm's failure to provide the client a full and final disbursement which is inferentially required per Chapter 23.3.

An additional comment regarding the fees is in order. During the post-trial hearing addressing fees, Judge Sparr asked Mr. Killmer some rather pointed questions about who would end up with the money assuming that he, Judge Sparr were to award §1988 attorney's fees. The exchange went like this:

> The Court: So what you are basically saying is the fees under which the lodestar under the statute are basically additional damages against the Defendant.
> Mr. Killmer: From the Defendant's perspective it probably looks that way because it means they have to write an additional check for that amount. The Supreme Court case law is that hte attorney's fees awarded under section 1988 are fees to the Plaintiff rather than to the law firm, so they wouldn't be writing the check to us. It is functionally equivalent.
> The Court: If you think that's the law, then I believe maybe you have answered my question. If the fees awarded today will be awarded to the Plaintiff and not to you, then your fees are obviously reflecting the fees that go tot he Plaintiff, have nothing to do with your Contingent Fee Agreement. Is that what you are telling me?
> Mr. Killmer: That's the law, yes.

In the Fee Agreement, the firm made it clear that, contrary to the representation to Judge Sparr, it would receive a 35% fee out of the additional award.

Since the law firm drafted the fee agreement with no client input, the fee agreement must be strictly construed against the attorneys. In dealing with it, the lawyers, however, have been dealing very aggressively with their clients. In this regard, their actions have been inconsistent with their fiduciary obligation.

II. PRACTICE ISSUES

As opposed to fiduciary questions which involve breaches of standards of conduct, traditional professional negligence questions involved breaches of standards of care. In addressing questions of this ilk, I have broken down the case into three separate categories of deficiencies, pleadings problems, discovery/trial presentation questions and client advice matters.

Perhaps the greatest shortcoming in the attorneys' handling of the case stemmed from their failure to object to the timeliness of the Defense's Rule 50 (b) Motion. In suggesting that this was the greatest error, by no means do I intend to imply that it was particularly egregious in terms of the lawyers' conduct, but the effect of this deficiency had the greatest negative impact on their clients. Rule 50 (b) Motions have to be filed within ten days after the judgment. The Defendants' Motion was not filed within this time frame. There was not an objection to the late filing. As a consequence, the timing objection was deemed waived. In the Tenth Circuit's opinion, the majority made this observation in a footnote:

> The Plaintiffs argue that Defendants failed to raise the issue of insufficient evidence to support punitive damages in their Fed. R. Civ. P 50(a) Motions, and therefore should not have been allowed to raise the issue in a Fed. R. Civ. P. 50 (b) Motion, or on appeal. However, the Plaintiffs themselves failed to object on this basis in their response to the Defendants' Rule 50 (b) Motion. Under such circumstances, the Plaintiffs may not assert the failure of the Defendants to raise the insufficient evidence issue. When the non-moving party fails to raise the inadequacy of a Rule 50 (a) Motion in opposition to a Rule 50 (b) Motion, that party cannot raise waiver as an argument on appeal. See Williams v. Runyon, 130 F.3d 568, 572 (3d Cir. 1997); Thompson & Wallace of Memphis, Inc. v. Falconwood Corp., 100 F.3d 429, 435 (5th Cir. 1996); Whelan v. Abell, 48 F.3d 1247, 1251-53 (D.C. Cir. 1995): Gibeau v. Nellis, 18 F.3d 107, 109 (2d Cir. 1994); Collins v. Illinois, 830 F.2d 692, 698 (7th Cir. 1987); Beauford v. Sisters of Mercy Province of Detroit, Inc., 816 F.2d 1104, 1108 n. 3 (6th Cir. 1987); Halsell v. Kimberly Clark Corp., 683 F.2d 285, 293-95 (8th Cir. 1982). Therefore, we will address the issue.

Had there been an appropriate objection to the Defendants' Rule 50(b) Motion, Judge Sparr could not have wiped out Ms. Foote's personal judgment as he did in granting the Motion. The entirety of the original judgment would have been preserved subject to the new trial motion and subsequent appeal.

000433

The second pleading deficiency relates to the same subject: Plaintiffs' counsel had stipulated to a Pre-Trial Order which did not include reference to Ms. Foote's personal claim. This deficiency served to provide Judge Sparr a legal basis on which to eliminate the personal award in granting the subsequent Rule 50 (b) Motion.

In my opinion, if these pleading deficiencies had not occurred, the Appeal would likely have gone very differently. And, even if remittitur had been the ultimate outcome on Appeal, the posture of the case in terms of a re-trial would have been significantly enhanced.

Next, turning to the question of discovery and trial presentation, I would be remiss if I did not, at the outset, compliment Mssrs. Killmer and Miller on their discovery and trial presentation with respect to the underlying liability. Where they let their clients down was on the damages side of the case. In this respect, there were two fundamental flaws.

As was evident from the Pre-Trial Order, Ms. Foote's counsel failed to appreciate and develop significant evidence pertaining to the emotional distress she endured as a consequence of the conduct of the Tabor Center and its agent. Ms. Foote's Kaiser chart is replete with references to stress and depression spawned by the personal affront from Tabor Center's representatives. Anti-depressant medication was prescribed. Had Ms. Foote's physicians been endorsed and called, the evidence undoubtedly would have had a great impact on the jury. And the Circuit's finding of no personal damages would have been rendered impossible.

The second damages discovery/presentation problem stemmed from the inadequacy of proof as to future lost profits. During the trial, Plaintiffs' counsel tried to shore up this deficiency with Mr. Kaempfer, but the Defendants' counsel quickly realized where this was headed and, at his request, Judge Sparr shut it down and admonished the jury to disregard Mr. Kaempfer's testimony on this subject.

My final standard of care criticisms pertain to the lawyers' inadequately involving their clients in the litigation, particularly with respect to settlement. Ms. Foote informs me that, for the most part, her contact was relegated to an intern. She believed that with respect to settlement her lawyers objectives were at odds with her own. And, from the correspondence, it is apparent that the lawyers' inadequately assessed the true extent of their clients' damages.

Where, as in this case, the jury's verdict is outside of an attorney's expectations – whether high or low -- the standard of care requires that post-trial settlement be explored, at least. There is nothing in the file to suggest that it was or, more importantly, that this option was ever explored with the clients.

III.
CONCLUSION

It is my opinion that the lawyers breached the standard of care as well as their fiduciary obligation to their clients. As a result, the clients ended up with a result which was significantly less than they otherwise would have achieved.

Sincerely,

Patric J. LeHouillier

PJL/kdp

LEHOUILLIER
& ASSOCIATES

ATTORNEYS AT LAW
PATRIC J. LEHOUILLIER*

*ALSO ADMITTED IN NEW YORK

90 SOUTH CASCADE
SUITE 1430
COLORADO SPRINGS, COLORADO 80903-1619
TELEPHONE 719 471-1330
FAX 719 473-3292

February 2, 2005

Charles Welton, Esq.
The Brock House
1800 Gaylord Street
Denver, CO 80206

Re: Foote & The Africa House v. Killmer et al.

Dear Mr. Welton:

I have now taken the opportunity to review the depositions of Mr. Killmer, Mr. Miller and Mr. Keaempfer. In addition, I have gone through all of post-trial pleadings which were filed in the United States District Court and, although there are a number of additional documents which I have requested, I did want to give you a supplemental report outlining a couple of additional conclusions which I have now reached.

Without question, the most significant supplemental conclusion - and it may well be the most significant conclusion of all - is that the Defendants failed to secure the equitable relief to which their clients were entitled.

I was struck by Mr. Killmer's deposition testimony concerning the pretrial settlement negotiations. From this testimony, it was clear that Ms. Foote's paramount objective was to achieve an acknowledgment by the Defendants that they had treated her inappropriately on account of her race. Failing that, she wanted her day in court; if the Defendants were not going to acknowledge that they had wronged her, she wanted a jury's validation.

A close second in Ms. Foote's list of priorities was to return to her original space in the shopping center where her business had been doing quite well.

CC0501

MARGARET EAGAN, M.D.
INTERNAL MEDICINE
ENDOCRINOLOGY
BOARD CERTIFIED

August 13, 2004

RE:

To Whom It May Concern:

I have reviewed all of the medical records for Ms. Tseghe Foote from January 1996 to the present. She was a patient at Kaiser Permanente from January 1996 until approximately February 2002. She then was cared for at the Caritas Clinic from May 2002 until August 2003. Current she is a patient of mine and has been since February 2004.

Ms. Foote moved here from Africa in 1976. She started her own business (Africa House in the Tivoli Center) in 1986. When the Tivoli closed she moved her business to Cherry Creek on 3rd Avenue. After being pursued for 2 years she agreed to open another Africa House in the Tabor Center in September 1992. Business did so well that she closed the Cherry Creek store in 1993 and opened up another site on Wazee Street. In 1995 Ms. Foote took out a loan to purchase a large inventory from Africa, using her house and stores as collateral. During this time the Tabor Center had been bought by a new owner and in April 1996 Ms. Foote heard rumors that her lease would not be renewed. In October 1996, while she was looking for new space, she was evicted. She hired a lawyer and the eviction was stopped. Ms. Foote was then able to move to a much larger and a much less desirable location in the Tabor Center. She hired a new law firm in January 1997 and it took until December 1998 to go to trial. During these 2 years Ms. Foote was reducing prices in her store to liquidate as much inventory as possible so she could pay off her loan. In February 1999 she was awarded $2.85 million. However, in approximately January 2001 she was told by the Tabor Center to move out. She closed her store in July 2001. In July 2002 her award was decreased to $75,000 which resulted in settlement of the lawsuit.

Ms. Foote has been under extreme emotional stress for the last 8 years. Prior to 1996 she was a healthy active 41-year-old female. Since October 1996 to the present she has been seen acutely by physicians 15 times. Most of these visits were due to a stress reaction. She has had weight loss down to 89 lbs; tachycardia with a pulse ranging from 100 to 140 beats per minute; hypertension with a blood pressure ranging 130-154/90-103; insomnia, chest pain, tremors, and headache. Ms. Foote has been on high blood pressure medications, anxiety medications, antidepressant medications, and antithyroid medications. She was even treated with radioactive iodine for presumptive Graves' disease, made hypothyroid, and placed on permanent thyroid replacement with Synthroid.

In March 1999 she was diagnosed with early menopause at age 44, most likely brought on by extreme stress. Ms. Foote was placed on hormone replacement therapy but due to finances was unable to afford the medication and so has only taken it intermittently. In May 2004 she was diagnosed with osteoporosis partially due to estrogen deficiency brought on by intermittent treatment with medication. As a result, she is at a higher risk of vertebral and hip fractures than a postmenopausal woman with normal bone mineral density.

As can be seen, the extreme stress Ms. Foote has undergone over the last 8 years has taken its toll, not only emotionally, (depression and anxiety) but also physically, causing high blood pressure, palpitations, early menopause, and osteoporosis. I am unable to apportion the causes of the stress due to what I have stated above and including the discrimination, the lawsuit, waiting for the appeal, and the appeal result.

Sincerely,

Margaret A. Eagan, M.D.
MAE/dld

4500 E. 9TH AVENUE, SUITE 720 S. DENVER, COLORADO 80220 TELEPHONE (303) 355-3525 FAX (303) 355-0255

MARGARET A. EAGAN, M.D.

4500 E. 9TH AVENUE, SUITE 550 S.
DENVER, COLORADO 80220

PHONE: 303-394-9355
FAX: 303-355-0255

FOR Tseghe Foote DATE 2/25/05

℞ ADDRESS ____________

DISP: Pt. has Graves disease (h/o)
SIG: that has been exacerbated by REFILL ____ TIMES
a very difficult lawsuit that has
DISP: resulted in the closing ~~of her business~~,
SIG: premature menopause, osteoporosis REFILL ____ TIMES
+ HTN + extreme anxiety w/insomnia.
DISP: * Pt. has been unable to work
since 7/01 + case finally comes to
SIG: court (trial) in 4/05. Disability is REFILL ____ TIMES
of indefinite duration.

COLORADO LIC. NO. 33365

☐ DAW

[signature] M.D.

DISTRICT COURT, COUNTY OF DENVER STATE OF COLORADO Court Address: Denver City and County Building 1437 Bannock Street, Room 256 Denver, CO 80202	04 FEB 19 PM 4:48 ▲COURT USE ONLY▲
TSEGHE FOOTE and THE GUIDES, LTD. d/b/a THE AFRICA HOUSE, Plaintiffs, v. MILLER, LANE, KILLMER & GREISEN, LLP; DAVID H. MILLER; DAROLD W. KILLMER; and KILLMER & LANE, LLP, Defendants.	Case Number: 04CV1256 Courtroom 5 R/A
Charles Welton Attorney for Plaintiff Attorney Registration #5337 1800 Gaylord Street Denver, CO 80206 Phone Number: (303) 333-9800 Facsimile Number: (303) 322-9546	

COMPLAINT NG

Plaintiffs, as and for their claims against the Defendants, set forth as follows:

GENERAL ALLEGATIONS

1. Tseghe Foote (hereinafter "Foote") and The Guides, Ltd. d/b/a Africa House (hereinafter "Africa House"), collectively referred to as Plaintiffs have at all

pertinent times been residents of the City and County of Denver, State of Colorado.

2. Defendants Darold W. Killmer (hereinafter "Killmer") and David H. Miller (hereinafter "Miller") have at all times maintained their law practice within the City and County of Denver, State of Colorado. At the time these Defendants entered into their fee agreement with the Plaintiff and commenced to represent the Plaintiff, said Defendants engaged in the practice of law through the Defendant entity known as Miller, Lane, Killmer & Greisen, LLP (hereinafter "Law Firm"); however, prior to the conclusion of the task undertaken, on or before July 1, 2002, the Law Firm was dissolved and the individual lawyers practiced in separate follow-on entities, including Defendant Killmer & Lane, LLP through which Mr. Killmer continued his law practice and representation of the Plaintiff. Miller, for his part, inexplicably ceased active participation in representation of Plaintiff, without proper basis, authority, or notice. The law firm entities were maintained at all pertinent times within the City and County of Denver, State of Colorado.

3. Defendants Miller, Killmer and the Law Firm entered into a Contingency Fee Agreement to represent the Plaintiffs in federal court within the City and County of Denver, State of Colorado. A copy of the Contingency Fee Agreement prepared by Defendants for execution by Foote regarding the underlying litigation is attached as Appendix A.

4. At all pertinent times Foote was the sole owner of Africa House, a retail import shop engaged in the business of selling art and craft goods made in Africa, purchased and imported by Ms. Foote for sale through her shop.

5. The underlying case taken over by Defendants involved civil rights discrimination litigation against the owners and operators of a downtown Denver mall called The Tabor Center alleging racial discrimination, relative to Plaintiffs' leasehold interest in the Tabor Center, which impacted and eventually deprived Foote of her ability to engage in business downtown Denver and deprived Africa House of its ability to survive as a business entity.

6. Defendants represented the Plaintiffs in the referenced federal court litigation through trial, post trial proceedings, post trial appeal, remand to the district court and compromised settlement.

FIRST CLAIM FOR RELIEF
(Breach of Fiduciary Duty)

7. Defendants in their representation of Plaintiffs violated applicable standards of conduct and breached their fiduciary duties to the Plaintiffs in several

particulars, including, but not limited to, the following:

a. Failure to adequately define or appreciate the scope of the engagement;

b. Failure to adequately present the client with payment options for the retention relative to the scope of the engagement;

c. Failure to act in the best interests of Plaintiffs and meet minimum mandated standards as set forth in Chapter 23.3 of the Colorado Rules of Civil Procedure relating to a contingency fee agreement including the following particulars:

1) Failure to provide consistent and clarifying invoicing in light of tensions between the written agreement and verbal assurances;

2) Failure to comply with requirements relative to expenditure of costs;

3) Failure to provide a Disbursement Statement;

4) Favoring the Defendants over the Plaintiff in fee allocation; and

5) Taking advantage of Plaintiffs' inventory and Foote's dependency upon Defendants as her counsel.

d. Failure to conform time record submittals, made to the court as counsel for the Plaintiffs regarding attorneys fees, to contemporaneously recorded records of time expenditures;

e. Failure to match the representation to the needs and expectations of the Plaintiffs;

f. Misrepresentation to the federal judge regarding the nature of the fee agreement between Plaintiffs and Defendants and its impact upon distribution of attorneys fees awarded by the court;

g. Failing to put the Plaintiffs' interest over the Defendants' interests in fee-related issues;

h. Failure to advocate in Plaintiff's best interests in settlement negotiation processes and opportunities;

i. Failure to advise Plaintiffs of the risks attendant to the post trial proceedings;

j. Failure to adequately communicate with Plaintiff Foote;

k. Failure to adequately prepare the case;

l. Failure to provide an adequate accounting; and

m. Overreaching in dealing with Plaintiffs.

8. As a result of this state of circumstances Plaintiffs have incurred injuries, damages and losses including but not limited to those set forth below addressing the consequences of the negligent actions of Defendants. Plaintiff Foote's injuries from the fiduciary breaches include emotional and mental stress including anxiety, frustration, and depression, which had physical impact and consequences upon Plaintiff.

9. As a result of these circumstances, Plaintiffs seek damages from the Defendants including those set forth below as well as emotional and mental stress damages for Foote, comprising both economic loss, set forth below, and noneconomic loss by Foote pursuant to **C.R.S. §13-21-102.5.**

10. Additionally, Plaintiffs seek exemplary damages from these Defendants, and each of them pursuant to **C.R.S. §13-21-102** as the breach of the fiduciary duty was attended by circumstances of wilful and wanton conduct in failing to maintain sufficient contact with the Plaintiff Foote to attend to her needs and expectations, as reflected in the disconnect from the time of first addressing the scope of the engagement through trial preparation and trial which failed to adequately acknowledge and address the Plaintiffs' circumstances and through the post trial appeal process through which Defendants failed to adequately communicate and advocate in the best interests of Plaintiffs, all exhibiting a consistent pattern of wilful and wanton neglect, despite Plaintiff Foote's efforts to be heard.

SECOND CLAIM FOR RELIEF
(Negligence)

11. In the course of representing the Plaintiffs, the Defendants' course of conduct fell below the applicable standard of care and constituted negligence.

12. The actions of the Defendants which comprised negligence include the following:

a. Failure to include Foote's claims in the Pretrial Order;
b. Failure to timely request of the court that the pleadings conform to the evidence as allowed by the rules following testimony of Foote's claims;

c. Failure to timely object to Defendants' out-of-time motion for relief pursuant to Rule 50(b);

d. Failure to timely perceive the need for, to calculate, to endorse, and to include as damages future economic losses through expert analysis and testimony;

e. Failure to obtain, disclose, endorse or use at trial available evidence to adequately support Plaintiff Foote's claim for emotional and physical injury and punitive damages, as well as Plaintiff Africa House's claims for economic loss and punitive damages;

f. Failure to conform the scope of the undertaking and their advocacy to the expectations and needs of the Plaintiffs;

g. Failure to adequately warn Plaintiffs of post trial risks or take action in an effort to reach a final settlement in light of those risks; and

h. Failure to adequately account to Plaintiffs in the settlement process regarding costs and fees in accordance with the rule referenced above.

13. As a result of this course of conduct by the Defendants, Plaintiffs have sustained damages as follows:

a. Foote's loss of her ability to earn a living and provide a service to the community through the business of the Africa House;

b. Loss of the proceeds of the judgment (secured by an appeal bond) against the Defendants which included the following components:

1) $200,000.00 compensatory award to Foote;

2) $1,500,000.00 punitive damage award to Foote;

3) $150,000.00 compensatory award to Africa House;

4) $1,000,000.00 punitive damage award to Africa House;

5) An award of costs;

6) Interest; and

7) An award of attorneys fees.

c. Loss of future economic damages admitted by Defendants to be in an amount in excess of $375,000.00.

d. Loss of monies paid to and/or retained by Defendants for attorneys fees and costs attendant to their representation.

14. Instead, Plaintiffs' recovery was limited to a post-remand settlement, in the amount of [illegible] minus 35% charged Plaintiff by her counsel for attorneys' fees; minus funds retained by the attorneys to date for expended costs, unauthorized in accord with the rule referenced above; minus additional fees paid by Plaintiffs beyond the 35%; minus the value of goods taken from Plaintiffs by Defendants; and minus yet additional fees sought and retained by Defendants.

15. Defendants' negligence was a cause of damages sustained by Plaintiffs as set forth above for which Defendants are liable, as a result of which Defendants should return funds and value in kind paid by Plaintiffs to Defendants and/or retained by Defendants from Plaintiffs as either fees or costs.

THIRD CLAIM FOR RELIEF
(Accounting)

16. In accord with fiduciary duties, ethical standards and Rule requirements, Plaintiffs seek from these Defendants an accounting to date of all funds paid by Plaintiffs or retained by Defendants and each of them -- with the bases therefore, including but not limited to a disbursement statement as referenced above.

17. Throughout the course of the representation extensive art work and works of craft in Plaintiffs' shop for retail sale were taken by Defendants and their agents for use in decorating their various offices and/or homes. Neither credit nor accounting for items of value was provided to Plaintiffs by Defendants.

18. Plaintiffs seek from these Defendants an accounting of all the items from Plaintiffs' shop which were taken by Defendants and their agents and/or passed through their hands, regardless of where presently located, including information in the following particular categories:

a. Description;
b. Location by specific address;

c. Purported ownership;

d. Value;

e. Purported basis of value determination;

f. Amount paid to or credited to Plaintiffs for same; and

g. Access to said item for examination and photography.

19. Regarding cost expenditures and Defendants' recovery of same from Plaintiffs, an accounting of which items are claimed to have been those contemplated within the fee agreement; those made with prior written authorization together with proof therefore; and those outside either the fee agreement or the requirement of prior written authorization.

FOR THESE REASONS Plaintiffs seek entry of judgment in favor of Plaintiffs and against the Defendants for damages and exemplary damages stemming from the breach of fiduciary duty as set forth in the First Claim for Relief and for damages stemming from the negligence as set forth in the Second Claim for Relief, against each Defendant, jointly and severally in accord with the provisions of **Rule 265(IA)(4)** of the Colorado Court Rules regarding professional service companies, providing for such joint and several liability against these Defendants, interest as allowed by statute, **C.R.S., 13-21-101**, and costs as allowed by statute and rule.

PLAINTIFFS REQUEST A JURY TRIAL.

Respectfully submitted,

CHARLES WELTON, P. C.

By: ______________________
Charles Welton, Reg. No. 5337
Attorney for Plaintiffs

<table>
<tr><td colspan="2">DISTRICT COURT, COUNTY OF DENVER, COLORADO
Court Address: Denver City and County Building
1437 Bannock Street, Room 256
Denver, CO 82020</td><td rowspan="3">▲COURT USE ONLY▲

____</td></tr>
<tr><td>Plaintiff:</td><td>THE GUIDES, LTD. d/b/a AFRICA HOUSE</td></tr>
<tr><td>Defendants [and Counterclaim Plaintiff]:</td><td>v.
MILLER, LANE, KILLMER & GREISEN, LLP; DAVID H. MILLER; DAROLD W. KILLMER; and KILMER & LANE, LLP</td></tr>
<tr><td colspan="3">SPECIAL VERDICT FORM B</td></tr>
</table>

DO NOT ANSWER THIS SPECIAL VERDICT FORM B IF YOUR FOREPERSON HAS COMPLETED SPECIAL VERDICT FORM A AND ALL JURORS HAVE SIGNED IT.

We, the jury, present our Answers to Questions submitted by the Court, to which we have all agreed:

1. Did the plaintiff, The Guides, Ltd. have damages or losses? (Yes or No)

ANSWER: yes

2. Were the defendants Miller, Lane, Killmer & Greisen, LLP, David H. Miller; Darrold W. Killer; and Killmer & Lane, L.L.P., negligent? (Yes or No)

ANSWER: yes

3. Was the negligence, if any, of the defendants a cause of any of the damages or losses claimed by the plaintiff? (Yes or No)

ANSWER: yes

4. Did the defendant breach any fiduciary duty to the plaintiff? (Yes or No)

ANSWER: yes

5. Was the breach of fiduciary duty, if any, a cause of damages or losses claimed by the plaintiff? (Yes or No)

ANSWER: Yes

If you find that the plaintiff did have damages or losses and you further find that the defendants were negligent and that such negligence was a cause of any of the plaintiff's damages or losses, then answer the following question.

6. What is the total amount of damages or losses, if any, for plaintiff caused by defendants' negligence?

ANSWER: $176,600.00

If you find that the plaintiff did have damages or losses and you further find that the defendants breached a fiduciary duty and such breach of fiduciary duty was a cause of any of plaintiff's damages or losses, then answer the following question:

7. What is the total amount of damages or losses, if any, for plaintiff caused by defendants' breach of fiduciary duty?

ANSWER: $13,924

Foreperson

COLORADO COURT OF APPEALS

Court of Appeals No.: 05CA1876
City and County of Denver District Court No. 04CV1256
Honorable Catherine A. Lemon, Judge

The Guides, Ltd., d/b/a The Africa House,

Plaintiff-Appellant,

v.

Miller, Lane, Killmer & Griesen, LLP; David H. Miller; Darold W. Killmer; and Killmer & Lane, LLP,

Defendants-Appellees.

JUDGMENT AFFIRMED

Division III
Opinion by: JUDGE KAPELKE*
Roy and Bernard, JJ., concur

NOT PUBLISHED PURSUANT TO C.A.R. 35(f)
Announced: June 14, 2007

Anne Whalen Gill, L.L.C., Anne Whalen Gill, Sharlene J. Aitken, Castle Rock, Colorado, for Plaintiff-Appellant

White & Steele, P.C., Kurt A. Horton, John M. Palmeri, Denver, Colorado, for Defendants-Appellees

*Sitting by assignment of the Chief Justice under provisions of Colo. Const. art. VI, § 5(3), and § 24-51-1105, C.R.S. 2006.

Plaintiff, The Guides, Ltd., d/b/a The Africa House, appeals the judgment entered by the trial court in favor of defendants, Miller, Lane, Killmer & Greisen, LLP; David H. Miller; Darold W. Killmer; and Killmer & Lane, LLP. We affirm.

I. Background

Plaintiff owned a retail store that specialized in African arts. The co-plaintiff, Tseghe Foote, was the sole owner and president of plaintiff. Plaintiff was the tenant under a month-to-month lease for retail space within the Tabor Center in Denver. In October 1996, the landlord terminated the lease.

A. Underlying Federal Case

In November 1996, plaintiff and the co-plaintiff filed an action in the United States District Court, asserting claims of racial discrimination against the landlord. Defendants represented plaintiff and the co-plaintiff in that action on a contingent fee basis. In 1999, following trial, the jury returned a verdict in favor of plaintiff and the co-plaintiff and awarded plaintiff $150,000 in compensatory damages and $1 million in punitive damages. The separate award in favor of the co-plaintiff was set aside by the federal district court.

On appeal, the Tenth Circuit of Appeals reduced plaintiff's damage award to $75,316.95, and remanded the case to the district court with directions that plaintiff could either accept the reduced award or have a new trial. Guides, Ltd. v. Yarmouth Group Prop. Mgmt., Inc., 295 F.3d 1065 (10th Cir. 2002).

In 2003, the parties in that action reached a settlement in the amount of [illegible] Under the terms of the settlement, plaintiff received [illegible] of which was disputed and placed in escrow), and its attorneys, defendants here, received [illegible]

B. State Malpractice Case

In April 2004, plaintiff and the co-plaintiff brought a state court action against defendants, alleging professional negligence and breach of fiduciary duty relating to their representation in the federal case. Defendants counterclaimed, asserting that the $32,000 in escrow was properly payable to them as costs, expenses, and attorney fees. The co-plaintiff's claims were later dismissed. Following trial, the jury returned a verdict in favor of plaintiff, awarding $176,600 on the negligence claim and $13,924 on the claim for breach of fiduciary duty.

The trial court held a post-trial hearing to address the

application of a setoff with respect to the previous settlement and defendants' counterclaim. At the conclusion of the hearing, the trial court applied a setoff of against the jury verdict, resulting in a zero award to plaintiff. The court also found for defendants on their counterclaim, awarding them $18,076, plus interest, of the $32,000 in escrow. Plaintiff received the remaining $13,924, plus interest.

II. Setoff

Plaintiff contends that the trial court erred in applying the settlement amount as a setoff against the jury verdict. We disagree.

Initially, we decline to address plaintiff's argument that the court erred in allowing the setoff because it was not pleaded as an affirmative defense. That argument was not raised in the trial court, and arguments not presented to, considered by, or ruled upon by the trial court will not be considered on appeal. See Estate of Stevenson v. Hollywood Bar & Cafe, Inc., 832 P.2d 718, 721 n.5 (Colo. 1992).

A. Jury Instruction Regarding Settlement

Contrary to the position it took in the trial court, plaintiff now contends on appeal that the trial court acted improperly in failing to instruct the jury in accordance with Greenemeier v. Spencer, 719 P.2d 710, 714-15 (Colo. 1986). We disagree.

In Greenemeier, the supreme court held that a trial court should bring to the jurors' attention the fact of settlement between a joint tortfeasor and an injured plaintiff in order to make them aware that any damage award would be apportioned properly among the defendants and the settling parties. Plaintiff contends that the trial court should have, sua sponte, given this instruction to the jury.

A trial court has a duty to instruct the jury correctly on the law applicable to the case. Genova v. Longs Peak Emergency Physicians, P.C., 72 P.3d 454 (Colo. App. 2003). However, counsel has a duty to examine the jury instructions and call the court's attention to any errors before the instructions are given to the jury. Failure to do so generally operates as a waiver of the right to seek appellate review of the propriety of a jury instruction. See C.R.C.P. 51; Bear Valley Church of Christ v. DeBose, 928 P.2d 1315 (Colo. 1996).

Here, plaintiff neither tendered nor requested a Greenemeier instruction. Nor did plaintiff contemporaneously object to the court's instructions on this basis. Rather, throughout trial, and until the post-trial hearing, plaintiff took the position that a Greenemeier instruction was inappropriate and should not be given under the circumstances here.

We therefore conclude that plaintiff has waived any objection to the instructions in this regard. See Bear Valley Church of Christ v. DeBose, supra; Curragh Queensland Mining Ltd. v. Dresser Indus., Inc., 55 P.3d 235, 242 (Colo. App. 2002).

B. Application of Setoff

Plaintiff contends that the trial court's application of the setoff was erroneous. We conclude that, under the doctrine of invited error, plaintiff is barred from raising this issue on appeal.

The doctrine of invited error prohibits a party from complaining of an error he or she intentionally invited or injected into the case. The doctrine applies where a party asks the court to take a particular action and later objects to that same action, and also where one party expressly acquiesces to conduct by the court or the opposing party. Horton v. Suthers, 43 P.3d 611 (Colo. 2002).

Here, the record reveals – and plaintiff concedes – that plaintiff acquiesced to the setoff throughout the proceedings in the trial court. First, in pretrial pleadings, plaintiff specifically raised the application of a setoff in its amended categorization of damages: "The damages are against a credit for the settlement amount received by Ms. Foote: minus the $32,000.00 which Defendants seek . . . leaving a total of to Ms. Foote."

Second, the parties' trial management order, approved by the court, conceded that "[t]he damages are against a credit for the settlement amounts."

Finally, in closing argument, plaintiff emphasized to the jurors that a setoff would occur after they returned their verdict:

> [If] you read the instructions, you see, and I better tell you, that the way the Court is doing this, there's no subtraction in this damage calculation for the settlement. The Court will do that later, so I hope you understand that it's not in there anywhere. . . . [The lost value of the business] is the number you're to plug in, and the Court will take into consideration later what to do with the settlement process.

Therefore, because plaintiff acquiesced to the court's applying a setoff based on the amount of plaintiff's prior settlement, the doctrine of invited error precludes plaintiff from raising this issue on appeal.

To the extent plaintiff asserts that the jury must have made a net award of damages, we reject this position as being wholly inconsistent with the jury instructions, which required the jury to consider and return a verdict on "the total amount of damages or losses." We must presume that the jury followed the instructions, see Lexton-Ancira Real Estate Fund, 1972 v. Heller, 826 P.2d 819 (Colo. 1992), and the record does not indicate to the contrary.

Finally, because it was raised for the first time on appeal, we decline to consider plaintiff's argument that the court used the wrong monetary amount in applying the setoff. See Estate of Stevenson v. Hollywood Bar & Cafe, Inc., supra.

III. Award of Costs

Plaintiff next contends that the trial court erred in denying it an award of costs as the prevailing party. We disagree.

C.R.C.P. 54(d) provides for an award of costs "to the prevailing party unless the court otherwise directs." A "prevailing party" is one who prevails on a significant issue in the litigation and derives some of the benefits sought by the litigation. Pastrana v. Hudock, 140 P.3d 188 (Colo. App. 2006). The number of claims upon which a party prevails and the amount awarded on those claims are not necessarily determinative of who the prevailing party is for purposes of awarding costs. Mackall v. Jalisco Int'l, Inc., 28 P.3d 975 (Colo. App. 2001).

An award of costs pursuant to C.R.C.P. 54(d) is committed to the discretion of the trial court and will be disturbed only if it is manifestly arbitrary, unreasonable, or unfair. Archer v. Farmer Bros. Co., 90 P.3d 228 (Colo. 2004). Even if each of the parties he could arguably be viewed as having prevailed in part, the award of costs in such a situation is still committed to the sole discretion of the trial court. Mackall v. Jalisco Int'l, Inc., supra.

Plaintiff suggests that it is the prevailing party by virtue of the jury verdict in its favor and the amount of the award. As the court noted in its order and judgment, however, defendants prevailed on their request for judgment in their favor, as well as on their counterclaim. The court declined to award costs to either party.

C.R.C.P. 54(d) does not require any cost award if "the court otherwise directs." Here, as each party prevailed in part, the court acted well within its discretion.

In light of our disposition, we need not consider defendants' renewed motion to dismiss.

The judgment is affirmed.

JUDGE ROY and JUDGE BERNARD concur.